Business-Driven IT-Wide Agile (Scrum) and Kanban (Lean) Implementation

An Action Guide for Business and IT Leaders

Business-Driven IT-Wide Agile (Scrum) and Kanban (Lean) Implementation

An Action Guide for Business and IT Leaders

Andrew T. Pham and David K. Pham

Foreword by Jack Bergstrand,
Former CFO of the Coca-Cola Beverages and CIO of the Coca-Cola Company

Foreword by Adam Warner, IT Management, ESC

CRC Press
Taylor & Francis Group
Boca Raton London New York

CRC Press is an imprint of the
Taylor & Francis Group, an **informa** business

A PRODUCTIVITY PRESS BOOK

CRC Press
Taylor & Francis Group
6000 Broken Sound Parkway NW, Suite 300
Boca Raton, FL 33487-2742

© 2013 by Taylor & Francis Group, LLC
CRC Press is an imprint of Taylor & Francis Group, an Informa business

No claim to original U.S. Government works

Printed in the United States of America on acid-free paper
Version Date: 20120726

International Standard Book Number: 978-1-4665-5748-2 (Paperback)

Library of Congress Cataloging-in-Publication Data

Pham, Andrew Thu.
    Business-driven IT-wide agile (scrum) and Kanban (lean) implementation : an action guide for business and it leaders / Andrew Thu Pham, David Khoi Pham.
       p. cm.
       Summary: "This book explains how to successfully deploy Agile and Kanban on a large scale in order to increase IT delivery capabilities. It factors in change, communication, a sense of urgency, clear and measurable goals, political realities, and infrastructure needs, all of which are critical ingredients for success. Through real world examples, the authors explain how IT-wide Agile and Kanban can be implemented to the entire enterprise and IT department. The text also includes many templates for use as an on-the-job guide for business and IT leaders and their teams. "-- Provided by publisher.
       Includes bibliographical references and index.
       ISBN 978-1-4665-5748-2 (pbk.)
       1. Agile software development. 2. Project management. 3. Information technology. I. Pham, David Khoi. II. Title.

    QA76.76.D47P487 2012
    005.1--dc23   2012027060

Visit the Taylor & Francis Web site at
http://www.taylorandfrancis.com

and the CRC Press Web site at
http://www.crcpress.com

To Jessica, Tiffany, and Kym, with love

Contents

Foreword

In our globally competitive and fast-changing business world, better and more productive projects are to the twenty-first century what better assembly lines were to the twentieth century. Unfortunately, the conventional project management approach fails to deliver on management's initial goals an alarming 70% of the time. Then enter Agile (Scrum) and, more increasingly, Kanban (Lean) with all the benefits they bring along.

Imagine how much better your software team's work would be if you were continually able, in some cases, to act on what team members did yesterday, what they are going to do today, and whether or not there are any obstacles to solve. Also, imagine how much better it would be, in other cases, if you could help improve your software team's work by not introducing a completely new process to the team, but instead visualized their current process while trying to optimize it with proven approaches—Kanban, among others—coming from the best just-in-time system in the world, the Toyota Production System (TPS).

As a logical sequence to their first book, *Scrum in Action: Agile Software Project Management and Development*, which is geared toward project teams, Andrew Pham and David Pham's new book is decidedly geared toward business and information technology (IT) executives who would like to know how to successfully deploy Agile (Scrum) and/or Kanban (Lean) on a large scale to IT in their effort to increase their teams' software delivery capability.

As a former CFO of the Coca-Cola Beverages and CIO of the Coca-Cola Company, I truly appreciate Andrew Pham and David Pham for having developed in this book a comprehensive and easy-to-follow guide for busy executives. Likewise, I also truly appreciate the fact that the authors' approach also factors in change, communication, a sense of urgency, clear and measurable goals, political realities, and infrastructure needs—all critical ingredients for success.

Rather than blindly deploy Agile as has been the trend during the past few years, the authors rightly suggest that we should first assess the environment and identify the organization's business goals first. Only then will we know what Agile (Scrum) and/or Kanban (Lean) concepts or techniques we need and how to combine them most effectively to solve our enterprise's problems.

In my book, *Reinvent Your Enterprise*, I wrote that speed is the new quality—with a spirit of action, imperfection, forgiveness, and continuous improvement needed. I am glad that Andrew Pham and David Pham's approach also factors in a similar type of purposeful adaptation—to deliver results by establishing a clear set of goals, assessing the environment, coming up with creative solutions that are more often than not a combination of Agile and Lean, regularly inspecting the execution's progress, and rapidly acting on lessons learned as well as adapting to the business's external environment or change in business strategy.

Incorporating Agile (Scrum) and Kanban (Lean) principles and practices into your software development organization on a large scale and in a creative way will go a long way toward increasing value and reducing risks. For this reason alone, you will find it—as I do—very worthwhile to spend time reading this very practical book.

Jack Bergstrand
CEO, Brand Velocity, Inc.
Author of Reinvent Your Enterprise
Former CFO of the Coca-Cola Beverages and CIO of the Coca-Cola Company
October 2011

Foreword

Perhaps you're a software development director or manager who has implemented Agile or Scrum successfully in your team. Then your boss, the CIO, comes to you and says, "Your team runs so efficiently with Agile—let's implement it across the whole IT department!"

At first you heartily agree and are excited by the challenge and the opportunity to drive improvement—but then reality sets in. Other groups have much different processes that may not easily adapt to Scrum. The data warehouse manager complains that she has constraints that can allow only a linear development flow—requirements analysis, data modeling, ETL, report development, user acceptance—that easily spans more than one sprint time frame. She is highly resistant to the change and has already started to complain to the CIO. And what about customer support? They never know what they might be working on today much less tomorrow or the next three weeks. How would Scrum possibly apply to them? Maybe this Kanban approach you've heard of would work? What's the right answer?

At this point hopefully you've come across this book by Andrew Pham and David Pham. By reading the book, you can see their practical experience in advising organizations in the move to Agile and Kanban (Lean) project management and software development processes.

First of all, they hammer home the timeless point that the focus of any IT improvement effort must be to improve the business, not merely to improve IT for IT's sake. They never cease, and rightly so, to remind the reader that IT exists to serve the business and that all IT improvement efforts must be framed in terms of business goals.

From my experience in several Fortune 500 firms, I have seen personally (on both sides) what happens when corporate IT departments don't put the needs of the business first. Namely, the business unit becomes disenchanted and hires its own IT staff. Corporate IT will lose funding sources and start to wither. It will constantly struggle to apply corporate standards and security controls on the rogue groups. Ultimately the company's bottom line will suffer because the business units are not leveraging the economies of scale and strategic advantage that a corporate IT group can offer.

So, instead of IT-centered goals such as "increase on-time delivery of IT projects by 20%" (unless your company's business is IT project management), define the business need first and then define what IT needs to do to support the goal. For instance, "To improve on-time delivery of manufacturing orders, increase the rate of new feature delivery in the factory scheduling software project by 20% within six months." This is the type of logic and practicality that prevails in this book but is often missing in other books.

At the same time, the authors provide an excellent overview of both Agile and Kanban practice and help us understand that a one-size-fits-all IT improvement effort is likely doomed to fail.

Agile, with Scrum as its most common and well-known process, is best suited to software development efforts where features can be designed, built, and delivered by one non-specialized, cross-functional team working together. Typically these features can be completely designed, built, and delivered within the time frame of a two- to four-week sprint (though I and many others do use Scrum to deliver software features on longer multi-sprint time frames, particularly for data warehousing).

Lean, and its most frequent incarnation, Kanban, however, allows you to keep your existing process and specialists while still providing a framework for improvement. To this effect, the authors do a great job of detailing the origins of the Lean movement in manufacturing, and at Toyota in particular, highlighting the "seven wastes" that Lean tries to address. Although meant originally for a manufacturing context, these wastes apply to software "manufacturing" just as readily: defects, wait time, too many items in process, and unnecessary extra features, just to name a few. If this is your case, Kanban is a method you can apply to your existing process that limits work in progress (WIP) to optimize workflow and reduce lead time rather than the traditional sprints. To this point, it is not hard to see that Kanban might work better for a software development organization with specialized teams and a more sequential process flow, especially in the case of software support teams.

An industrial engineer by education who progressively became specialized in IT team management, I also appreciate the authors' initiative to create a new process framework (called the soccer process framework), as described in one of the case studies. Based on both Kanban (Lean) and Agile practices, it provides a process for larger project teams. It is guided by both a practical way to identify the same level of fine-grain requirements, and by an architectural vision, which is much needed for more complex software projects. As the authors rightly point out, both Agile and Lean (Kanban) have something to contribute to the diverse teams that make up an IT department; it is not an "all or nothing" proposition. The IT department must work closely with the business first to define the business goals and assess the environment, and then decide which processes will best meet the needs of the business.

On top of a very logical seven-step process for IT-wide software capability improvement, this book also includes comprehensive advice, plans, tools, and practical case studies. By reading the book, you will be well equipped to determine what's best for your IT organization. I am glad to have read it and now have it in my library.

Adam Warner
IT Management, Software Delivery
Education Service Center, Region 10
Richardson, Texas
October 2011

Preface: What Is This Book About?

The main objective of this book is to provide a practical guide to business and IT leaders who want to improve IT capability to better serve the business. By this, we mean the ability for IT teams to improve the pace at which software applications can be delivered, not just on one Agile pilot project but on all IT projects. But there lies the difficulty for IT management to make the leap from doing Agile or Kanban (Lean) on one project to an IT-wide effort, which requires much more than just deploying some Agile techniques to a few people.

Likewise, rather than blindly deploy Agile to the entire IT organization in a one-size-fits-all approach, we also show in this book how IT and business management can work together to determine business goals that can drive this IT-wide undertaking. IT improvement may also require leverage of Kanban (Lean), rather than of Agile alone, to improve its ability to deliver better and faster applications on a large scale.

While we make no claim that what we mention in this book is the best or the only way to introduce change programs into a company, everything in this book comes from our experience in software project management and software delivery in the trenches within companies of different sizes.

To make things easier for the busy IT leader and executive, we have constructed and included in this book a few case studies, with the intent to illustrate ideas or principles. All resemblance to a specific, real-life event or character is, therefore, purely coincidental.

It is, as always, up to the readers to devise approaches and ideas that will make the most sense in their specific situation.

Who Should Read This Book?

This book is for business executives, IT leaders, and senior staff interested in introducing Agile or Kanban (Lean) to IT departments on a large scale to better serve their business.

"A journey of a thousand miles begins with a single step."

Lao-tzu
Chinese philosopher

Acknowledgments

First, we thank our family for all their unwavering and unconditional love and support.

Next, our thanks go to Sharon Sukosolvisit, Sameer Bendre, Ben Oguntona, Raj Vollala, and Greg Johnson for discussions that led to several improvements in the book, and, in particular, to Jack Bergstrand, author of *Reinvent Your Enterprise*, former CFO of the Coca-Cola Beverages and CIO of the Coca-Cola Company, and to Adam Warner, who is part of IT management at the Education Service Center, Region 10 (Texas), for having reviewed our book and written the Forewords.

Next, we would like to thank the team at Productivity Press and, in particular, Kristine Mednansky, senior acquisitions editor and Iris Fahrer, project editor, for all their help.

Last but not least, our thanks go to all of the authors whose works are cited here. To those we have not mentioned, please know that we have made every effort to trace all of the ideas and copyright holders, but if any have been inadvertently overlooked, please let us or our publisher know so that we can make the necessary amendments at the earliest opportunity.

Andrew T. Pham
David K. Pham

About the Authors

Andrew T. Pham, author of *Scrum in Action: Agile Project Management and Software Development in the Real World*, has trained hundreds of software professionals and coached multiple project teams throughout the world to Agile (Scrum) and Kanban (Lean).

An elected senior member with the prestigious IEEE (Institute of Electrical and Electronics Engineers), Andrew Pham has held top positions in project management, enterprise architecture and software development.

In addition, Andrew Pham is also a PMP and PMI-ACP, the Project Management Institute's newly created certification for Agile Practitioner.

David K. Pham, prolific software creator, is the author of the two "Ruby on Rails" case studies in the book *Scrum in Action: Software Project Management and Development*, and a Sun-Certified Java and Microsoft-Certified Developer.

A technology entrepreneur, he is the former CTO of KTD Media Corp. and currently president of a web-based company based in Providence, Rhode Island.

David K. Pham was the invited guest speaker at the DevChatt conference for software developers in Nashville, Tennessee, in 2011.

SETTING UP THE STAGE 1

Chapter 1

Ineffectiveness of IT Software Project Management and Development: What Can We Do about It?

Even though much improvement has been made throughout the years (probably thanks to the introduction of new ideas and techniques), there is undoubtedly still a lot of room for improvement, particularly with regard to software project management and development.

Except for some companies where information technology (IT) has become so successful, the business within a company usually tend to perceive IT as a group of people who will take a long time and a lot of money to build a new software application for the business. Furthermore, when IT finally delivers the new software application or report, it often fails to meet the business needs of the company.

As a result, business becomes disenchanted with IT and goes on to create their own little IT shops, far too common still today, with a new army of newly hired developers. Although this helps meet the business needs in the short term, it disconnects business from the corporate IT tools, which results often in systems that are not as easily managed, secured, or controlled, without talking about the ever-expanding costs, for both people and software licenses.

For this reason, and to be looked at as a strategic partner, IT must recognize the utmost importance of being business driven and must change its practices accordingly. Likewise, businesses must also understand and appreciate the value of IT's expertise, assistance, and resources for the sustainability of their own livelihood, and therefore collaborate more and better with IT.

Why Are Command-and-Control and Waterfall Life Cycle Approaches Harmful When Used Together?

There are several reasons IT fails in software delivery, but there are two particular reasons, which are of major interest to us for the purpose of this book. The first reason is the waterfall software development life cycle, and the second is the command-and-control management style when they are used together.

The command-and-control management style may have helped manage work in the twentieth century, but when applied to today's knowledge workers, it is obvious that it is no longer effective. The reasons for this are multiple, but the obvious lack of motivation, lack of initiative, lack of teamwork (versus "everyone for himself"), and lack of collaboration are among the main reasons why it has failed.

As for the waterfall life cycle, as shown in Figure 1.1, the reason why it is not effective is mainly because of the following reasons:

1. Too much time is spent on detailing the plan and gathering requirements up front before design and coding can start.
2. If errors or omissions are uncovered, the sequential nature of the waterfall model does not allow the team to go back to the previous phase to make corrections; rather they must wait until the next cycle.
3. This type of sequential life cycle does not promote frequent interaction between the business users and the software development team, which understandably leads to misunderstanding and miscommunication.

Kanban (Lean) experts contend, and we agree with them, that the previously mentioned issues become less of a problem when the method is applied to software development on a smaller batch, as can be seen in Figure 1.2.

What Figure 1.2 shows is how the waterfall approach can work if we detail and develop only a few key requirements at a given point in time. By experience, this has turned out to be much more preferable to spending a

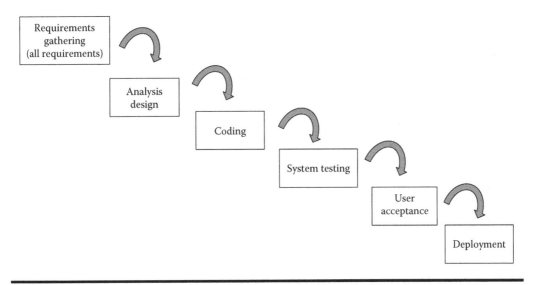

Figure 1.1   The waterfall software development life cycle (with large batch of requirements).

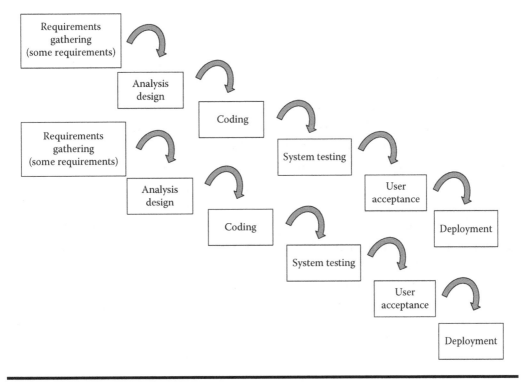

Figure 1.2   The waterfall software development life cycle (with smaller batch of requirements).

lengthy period, sometimes up to three or four months for instance, gathering and detailing all business requirements and confining them to a large document called a business requirements document (BRD). (We address this in greater detail later.)

For the previously mentioned reasons, when the waterfall approach and the command-and-control management style are applied together, they turn software project management and development into a difficult exercise, with few results. This is the reason why IT is often perceived within a company as a liability and a cost center, rather than the strategic enabler or a profit center it should be for the organization it is supposed to serve, public or private, profit or nonprofit.

What Can We Do about It?

Bothered by what they heard and saw, a group of software experts got together in 2001 at a ski resort in Utah to search for a better way to develop software. Out of that meeting, they drafted what has become known as the Agile Manifesto, the foundation of all of the Agile processes, including Scrum. Since then, Agile processes have turned many software development initiatives into successful endeavors, but over time, some Agile processes have revealed limitations.

In the meantime, Kanban as a Lean method applied to software development came about and has proven its worth in software support and maintenance, with some successful applications in software development, either as a complement or even a replacement of Agile processes.

To help readers clearly understand what Agile and Lean are, as well as learn the distinction and similarities between the two, the next chapter will review both Agile (including Scrum) and Kanban (as part of Lean), before we delve into the meat of our business-driven large-scale process improvement framework.

In the next chapter, we also review the reason why we consider Kanban to be the most promising Lean approach to software development.

Chapter 2

Executive Summary of Agile (Scrum) and Kanban (Lean)

In this chapter, we will try to first explain what Agile (Scrum) and Kanban (Lean) are before describing their differences and similarities.

So, What Is Agile?

Even if Scrum, one of the best-known Agile processes, was conceived before the Agile Manifesto was drafted, it is a well-known fact that the Agile Manifesto is the founding bedrock of the modern Agile movement.

So, what is the Agile Manifesto?

Agile Manifesto

In a nutshell, the Agile Manifesto reads as follows:

> We are uncovering better ways of developing software by doing it and helping others do it. Through this work we have come to value:
>
> - Individuals and interactions over processes and tools.
> - Working software over comprehensive documentation.
> - Customer collaboration over contract negotiation.
> - Responding to change over following a plan.

That is, while there is value in the items on the right, we value the items on the left more.[1]

> *Kent Beck, Mike Beedle, Arie van Bennekum, Alistair Cockburn, Ward Cunningham, Martin Fowler, James Grenning, Jim Highsmith, Andrew Hunt, Ron Jeffries, Jon Kern, Brian Marick, Robert C. Martin, Steve Mellor, Ken Schwaber, Jeff Sutherland, Dave Thomas*

Along with the four values, the Agile Manifesto is also comprised of twelve principles:

1. Our highest priority is to satisfy the customer through early and continuous delivery of valuable software.
2. Welcome changing requirements, even late in development. Agile processes harness change for the customer's competitive advantage.
3. Deliver working software frequently, from a couple of weeks to a couple of months, with a preference to the shorter time scale.
4. Business people and developers must work together daily throughout the project.
5. Build projects around motivated individuals. Give them the environment and support they need, and trust them to get the job done.
6. The most efficient and effective method of conveying information to and within a development team is face-to-face conversation.
7. Working software is the primary measure of progress.
8. Agile processes promote sustainable development. The sponsors, developers, and users should be able to maintain a constant pace indefinitely.
9. Continuous attention to technical excellence and good design enhances agility.
10. Simplicity—the art of maximizing the amount of work not done—is essential.
11. The best architectures, requirements, and designs emerge from self-organizing teams.
12. At regular intervals, the team reflects on how to become more effective, then tunes and adjusts its behavior accordingly.

One can deduct from these principles that the Agile process is any process or approach that favors frequent interaction between an empowered software development team and the business users, and which considers working software regularly delivered in increments as the only valid measure of a software project team's success and the only way to make sure that the software will meet its business users' requirements (by way of regular review and demo).

Example of a Known Agile Process: Scrum

Scrum is one of the best-known Agile processes. Originally invented in the early 1990s by Jeff Sutherland and Ken Schwaber, even before the formal meeting that led to the drafting of the Agile Manifesto, Scrum is naturally influenced, as mentioned earlier, by that meeting's discussion, since both Jeff Sutherland and Ken Schwaber attended the meeting.

As an Agile process framework, Scrum also favors a time-boxed incremental approach to software development and project management by advocating frequent interaction with the business during what is known as a *Sprint* (or *iteration* in simple Agile language).

In essence, there are three components to a Scrum project team, as shown in Figure 2.1: the product owner (PO), the ScrumMaster, and the development team.

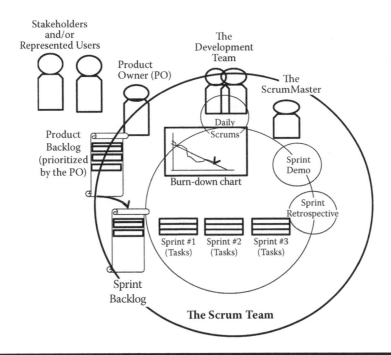

Figure 2.1   The essence of Scrum.

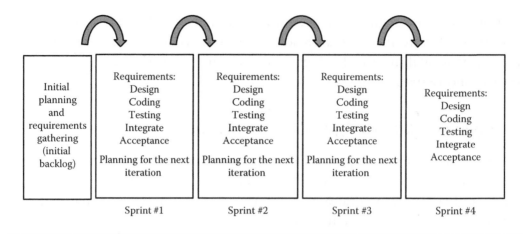

Figure 2.2   Sprint-based software development using Scrum.

Figure 2.1 shows that everything starts in Scrum with the PO, who, in a working relationship with both stakeholders and business users, identifies the requirements, which she or he will put in a product backlog before some of them are moved into a list of prioritized stories for the team to begin sprinting. The development team will work from this list, around short iterations called Sprints. Normally, a Sprint will last between one and four weeks, as can be seen in Figure 2.2.

Rather than meeting with business users only once every three or four months when there is a need for their sign-off, as in the old waterfall days, Scrum strongly suggests that the development team meet regularly, if not daily, not only with the users but also between themselves to check on their progression toward the Sprint's goal. This explains why the Agile team tries to have frequent, if not daily, working sessions with the users, and between themselves during a daily ceremony that is known as the daily standup or daily Scrum.

As things progress, the developers will reserve a few hours at the end of each Sprint to demonstrate, to the PO and key stakeholders or users, what they are able to build.

Unlike a traditional waterfall project, Scrum does not recommend that a detailed project plan is built with hundreds of tasks to keep track of the project team's progress. Instead, it only recommends that the team's progress is tracked by requirements and that the remaining work be kept updated in a report, called a burn-down chart, as seen in Figure 2.3, which shows that the project team is ahead of schedule. Figure 2.4 shows an example of a team behind schedule.

Given the managerial nature of this book, we have summarized here only a few key Agile practices. For more details on Agile or Scrum practices

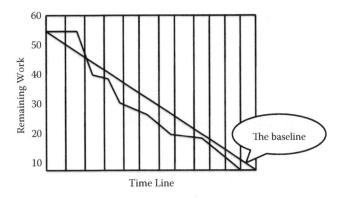

Figure 2.3   A burn-down chart showing the team ahead of schedule.

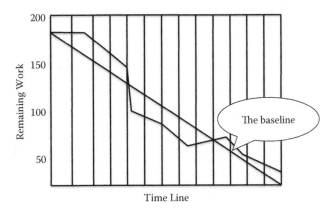

Figure 2.4   A burn-down chart showing the team behind schedule.

in the real world, please refer to our previous book, *Scrum in Action: Agile Software Project Management and Development.*[2]

Agile Practices in a Nutshell

Different people have different interpretations of what practicing Agile means, but in general, when a team says that they practice Agile, it means that they follow, more or less, the following practices:

1. Have frequent interaction with business users.
2. Empower teams to make their own commitment and decide how to organize their work around short iterations.
3. Inspect and adapt teamwork during daily team interaction.
4. Build and integrate often or even daily, if possible.
5. Deliver frequently.

Agile has been considered by some agilists as a good fit for all types of organizations and situations, at least, until recently. But that is, as we will see, a very partisan view and far from the reality in the trenches.

So, What Is Lean and What Is Kanban?

Originating from Japan during the formation of the Toyota Production System, Kanban[3] is a Lean method, based on visual cards, that states new work (request) should be accepted into the system only when there is available capacity to handle it. Because Kanban is part of the Lean techniques, we will review the fundamentals of Lean before taking a closer look at Kanban.

So, What Is Lean?

Lean is the English term—popularized by a team of researchers working under James Womack's direction from the Massachusetts Institute of Technology (MIT)—to describe the system known as the Toyota Way inside the company that created it. For practical purposes, in this book we will consider Lean as a catchword that describes a system approach to producing more with less by empowering employees and by minimizing waste.

To illustrate what waste is, let's review the seven types of waste that Shigeo Shingo[4] identified (along with co-creator Taiichi Ohno, the acknowledged father of Kanban):

1. Transportation

   The unneeded movement of products and/or materials between process steps is waste. Moving things between plants and floors can lead to damage and, most important, create no value for the customer.

   In software development, this could equate to the hand-off of some paper documentation from one team to the next.
2. Waiting

   Any time a worker is idle and waiting for something to do, he or she is wasting time.

   In software development, this happens when some members of the development team are free but do not have anything they can work on.

3. Overproduction

Producing more than what the market demands is waste and can lead to other waste, such as high material costs and expensive human resources.

In software development, this is what happens when the team produces features that are not really needed by the users, a phenomenon known as *silver plating*.

4. Defects

In software development, this is any deliverable that has errors and/or requires rework.

5. Inventory

Whenever inventory happens to exist along the assembly line, that is waste. Even if it may be needed, it is still non-value added.

In software development, this is what happens when there are artifacts throughout the life cycle that no one needs to use to create their production.

6. Motion

Any movement of employees that does not add anything to the process is waste.

In software development, this is any process step that requires an exchange between two team members that does not add anything to the overall process of value creation.

7. Extra processing

Any processing step that does not add any value to any artifact or product is waste.

In software development, this is what happens when team members have to do certain steps or things that do not directly contribute to the creation of value for the end users.

In addition to these seven types of wastes, an eighth form of waste has been added, which is the "underutilization of human resources."

Even though Lean has been mentioned for quite some time in software development, as witnessed by the writings of some early Lean authors,[5] there were no such Lean processes as Scrum or XP within the Agile space. All of this changed with David Anderson's first known attempt to apply Kanban to software development.[6]

So, What Is Kanban?

Without getting into the debate over the difference between Kanban with a capital *K* and kanban with a lowercase *k,* we will use the term *Kanban* with a capital *K* to indicate a new approach to software development using Lean concepts and techniques, including the famous Kanban cards, which originated from the Toyota Production System.

Unlike Agile, and Scrum in particular, Kanban does not require new roles such as PO or ScrumMaster. In all simplicity (which is its strength), Kanban allows an IT organization to keep all their current specialists (such as DBA, business analysts, testers, etc.) and continue to use their software development life cycle even if it is based on the waterfall approach. The reason why Kanban experts do not worry even when faced with a waterfall model is because it is the very premise of the Kanban approach to optimize using Lean concepts and techniques no matter what process a team is using.

Although different Kanban (Lean) practitioners have different ways of applying Kanban in software development, we believe the essence of how a software team uses Kanban consists of the following steps at the simplest level:

1. Visualize the current workflow
2. Capture current metrics and rules
3. Identify bottlenecks
4. Establish a new service level agreement (SLA) and policies
5. Limit work in progress (WIP)
6. Measure new lead times and some other metrics
7. Optimize

Let's review these seven points, one by one, in more detail.

1. Visualize the current workflow.
   Without a clear understanding of how the current process works and how work is actually performed, any discussion will be purely speculative. This is why the first step will be to visualize the workflow as soon as you can.

   For example, imagine that you are in an organization where the software life cycle looks somewhat like Figure 2.5.
2. Capture current metrics and rules.
   Without a good understanding of what the performance of the current process is and whether the business users are happy or not, any

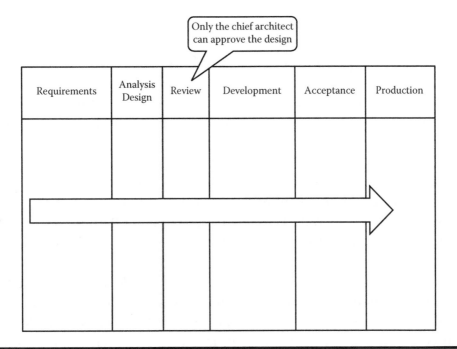

Figure 2.5   An example of a current workflow.

improvement attempt will be hazardous. Therefore, it will be key to capture rules as to what has been going on.

Examples of such rules could include the following:

   a. All requests are delivered between six and twelve weeks.

   b. No development will be allowed before the chief architect has given approval.

   c. All products should be tested by users before being released into the market.

   d. Some users are available only to perform user acceptance testing.

3. Identify bottlenecks.

By interviewing the team, as in this example, we came to realize that the chief architect represents a bottleneck, as seen in Figure 2.5, especially when he is not available or is so overloaded that he cannot perform his review on time.

4. Establish a new SLA and policies.

The intent behind the idea of SLA and policies is to identify the business customers' or users' expectations and what both sides should do to get to this new level of performance so that they can establish a trusting relationship.

For an example of SLA, we can imagine that the team will guarantee that all new requests will be delivered in less than six weeks. In return, the team could use this opportunity to require that the users be available three weeks before production to thoroughly test all the new features. In terms of new rules or policies, the team could decide that they should work on regulatory requests first and only take care of non-regulatory items after.

5. Limit work in progress (WIP).

Once the new SLA and mutual expectations have been reached, it will be time to review the team members' workload and see how to establish some limits on WIP. The idea behind limiting WIP is to set the number of requests for work a team can accept into the system without becoming overloaded.

To clarify this point, let's go through an example with some diagramming. Let's assume that we have a team of two business system analysts, three developers, three testers, and two technical writers. With three developers on the team, we can only have a maximum of three requirements being developed at any given time. To mark this limit, we write a number 3 into the upper right corner of the Development column, as in Figure 2.6.

Because development work normally takes longer than requirements and analysis, we can imagine that the order point (the point at which

Requirements	Analysis and Design	Development ⌐3	Acceptance	Production
Story 15	Story 11	Story 6	Story 4	Story 1
Story 14	Story 9 / Story 12	Story 7	Story 3	
Story 13	Story 10	Story 8	Story 5	Story 2

Figure 2.6 An example WIP.

Requirements	Analysis and Design	3	5	Development	3	Acceptance	Production
Story 16	Story 11			Story 8 / Story 6		Story 4	Story 1
Story 15	Story 12			Story 9		Story 3	
Story 14	Story 10 / Story 13			Story 7		Story 5	Story 2

Figure 2.7   An example of the concept of order point in Kanban.

the business analyst can pull one requirement into the Analysis and Design column to work on) will be 3, but the limit can be higher than 3—let's say 5 (as in Figure 2.7).

Now, before examining more advanced concepts in Kanban, let's assume that there are three members of the staff working on this project, which can be translated into three lanes as seen in Figure 2.8.

Requirements	Analysis and Design	Development	Acceptance	Production
Story 15	Story 11	Story 8 / Story 6	Story 4	Story 1
Story 14	Story 12	Story 9	Story 3	
Story 13	Story 10	Story 7	Story 5	Story 2

Figure 2.8   An example of the concept of swim lane in Kanban.

Requirements	Analysis and Design [3] [5]	Development [3]	Acceptance	Production
Story 15	Story 11	Story 8 Story 6	Story 4	Story 1
Story 14	Story 12	Story 9	Story 3	
Story 13	Story 10	Story 7	Story 5	Story 2

Figure 2.9   An example of the concept of queue.

By looking at Figure 2.8, we should remember that because we only have three developers, we should turn the Analysis and Design column from a pipeline into a queue, as in Figure 2.9. This allows a developer to work on any request that is in the queue, something they could not have done if the queue had stayed a pipeline only for a specific developer.

To make it easy for team members to know when an item will be ready to be pulled into the next column (station), a column can be divided into two sub-columns, one "ongoing" and one "done," as seen in Figure 2.10.

6. Measure new lead times and some other metrics.

Like in Scrum, the Kanban team also has a daily standup, but unlike the daily standup in Scrum, Kanban's daily standup focuses more on the workflow (to make sure that it is continuously moving) rather than on the Sprint's goal.

Before each daily standup, an update should be made to show the team's progress. The diagram that shows whether the lead time is improving or if there is an increase in throughput is called the *cumulative flow diagram* or *CFD* (Figure 2.11).

7. Optimize.

As part of our continuous effort to optimize the development team's work, we may be tempted to also organize the work around common data-related requirements to keep the work flowing, as shown in Figure 2.12.

Requirements	Analysis & Design		Development		Acceptance		Production
	3	**5**	**3**				
	Ongoing 3	Done	Ongoing 3	Done	Ongoing 2	Done	
Story 15 Story 13	Story 11		Story 8	Story 6	Story 4		Story 1
Story 14	Story 10	Story 12	Story 9		Story 5	Story 3	Story 2
			Story 7				

Figure 2.10   An example of "ongoing" and "done" on a Kanban board.

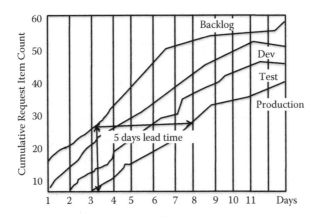

Figure 2.11   A cumulative flow diagram (CFD).

This would mean that the number of limits in the Development column could be increased to 6, as in Figure 2.13.

This is to say that the order point for the Analysis and Design column can also be increased from 6 to 9, as in Figure 2.14.

Eventually we could combine the Analysis and Design and Development columns to allow for more frequent customer interaction, as in Figure 2.15.

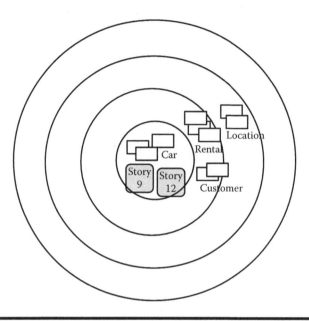

Figure 2.12 Organizing stories around common data elements.

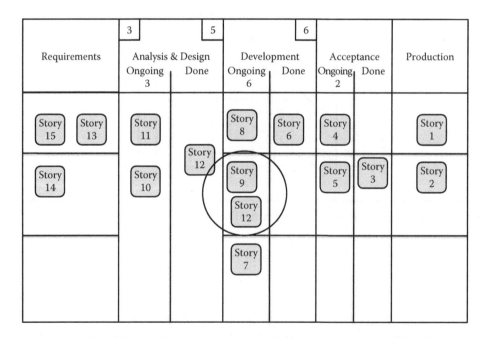

Figure 2.13 Kanban organized around common data elements.

Requirements	Analysis & Design		Development		Acceptance		Production
	6	9		6			
	Ongoing	Done	Ongoing	Done	Ongoing	Done	
	6		6		2		
Story 15 Story 13	Story 11		Story 8	Story 6	Story 4		Story 1
Story 14	Story 10		Story 9 Story 12		Story 5	Story 3	Story 2
			Story 7				

Figure 2.14 Increasing the previous order point in the Analysis and Design column.

Requirements	Analysis/Design/Development	Acceptance	Production
	6		
Story 16 Book	Story 11 Story 8 Story 6	Story 4	Story 1
Story 15 Reservation	Story 12 Story 9	Story 3	
Story 14 Patron	Story 10 Story 7 Story 13	Story 5	Story 2

Figure 2.15 Combining the Analysis and Design column with the Development column.

Kanban Practices in a Nutshell

Different people have different interpretations of what practicing Kanban means, but in general, when a team says that they practice Kanban, it normally means that they more or less do the following:

- Start with current process and keep all roles, titles, and responsibilities intact.
- Identify ways to measure current team performance.
- Identify bottlenecks and waste.
- Establish new policies and SLA.
- Limit WIP.
- Measure new results.
- Optimize.

Based on these practices, Kanban appears to be a continuous and evolutionary process of change and adaptation rather than a radical process change, as is the case with Agile or Scrum.

Similarities between Agile/Scrum and Kanban

Similarities between Agile and Kanban are shown in Figure 2.16, whereas the **differences** between Agile and Kanban are listed in Figure 2.17.

Some **similarities** between Scrum and Kanban are shown in Figure 2.18, and **differences** between Scrum and Kanban are shown in Figure 2.19.

So, what are the real differences and similarities between Agile and Kanban?

Agile	*Kanban*
1. Agile project manager	1. Software manager
2. Limit work at the iteration level	2. Limit work (WIP) at the state/phase level
3. Self-organized and empowered team	3. Team empowered to make decision on its own

Figure 2.16　Similarities between Agile and Kanban.

Agile	Kanban
1. Iteration	1. No iteration needed
2. User stories	2. No user stories needed
3. Generalist team	3. Specialist team is OK
4. New team structure and new roles (PO, Agile Master, development team)	4. No new team structure and no new roles (whatever exists)
5. Use velocity as the metric for process improvement	5. Use lead time as the metric for process improvement
6. New requirements (user stories) can only be added to the next iteration	6. Requirements can be added at any time whenever capacity is available
7. Almost new vocabulary, as in Scrum (Agile project manager, PO, development team)	7. Whatever current vocabulary is
8. Item size needs to be broken down to fit an iteration	8. No item size needs to be broken down
9. Agile board is reset (after each iteration)	9. Kanban board is persistent
10. Cross-functional team	10. Whatever team structure that exists

Figure 2.17   Differences between Agile and Kanban.

Scrum	Kanban
1. Limit work at the iteration level	1. Limit work (WIP) at the state/phase level
2. Self-organized and empowered team	2. Team empowered to make decision on its own

Figure 2.18   Similarities between Scrum and Kanban.

On the surface, it looks as if they are not very different, but deeper examination reveals that Agile puts greater focus on frequent interaction with the business customers and on regular software delivery. Kanban, on the other hand, starts with the current process and improves it gradually by limiting WIP and by systematically reducing waste and bottlenecks to reduce lead time and to increase throughput.

Scrum	Kanban
1. No project manager	1. Project manager is OK
2. Iteration	2. No iteration needed
3. User stories	3. No user stories needed
4. Generalist team	4. Specialist team is OK
5. New team structure and new roles (PO, ScrumMaster, development team)	5. No new team structure (no new roles)
6. Use velocity as the metric for process improvement	6. Use lead time as the metric for process improvement
7. User stories can only be added to the next Sprint	7. Requirements can be added at any time whenever capacity is available
8. New vocabulary	8. Whatever current vocabulary is
9. Items must be broken down to fit a Sprint	9. No item needs to be broken down
10. Scrum board is reset after every Sprint	10. Kanban board is persistent

Figure 2.19 Differences between Scrum and Kanban.

Summary

This chapter addressed the reasons why IT lacks efficiency in software project management and development, and why command-and-control management style and waterfall are harmful, especially when they are used together.

This chapter also laid the foundation behind the definitions of Agile (and Scrum) and Kanban (and Lean), and pointed out their similarities and differences.

Endnotes

1. Kent Beck, Mike Beedle, Arie van Bennekum, Alistair Cockburn, Ward Cunningham, Martin Fowler, James Grenning, Jim Highsmith, Andrew Hunt, Ron Jeffries, Jon Kern, Brian Marick, Robert C. Martin, Steve Mellor, Ken Schwaber, Jeff Sutherland, Dave Thomas. 2001. Snowbird, Utah. http://www.agilemanifesto. org/iso/en/ (accessed June 7, 2012).
2. Andrew Pham and Phuong-Van Pham, *Scrum in Action: Agile Project Management and Software Development* (Boston: Cengage, 2010).

3. Japanese Management Association, *Kanban, Just-in-Time at Toyota* (Stamford, CT: Productivity Press, 1985).
4. Shigeo Shingo, *A Study of the Toyota Production System from an Industrial Engineering Viewpoint* (Tokyo: Japan Management Association, 1981).
5. Mary Poppendieck and Tom Poppendieck, *Lean Software Development: An Agile Toolkit* (Boston: Addison-Wesley, 2003).
6. David Anderson, *Kanban* (Sequim, WA: Blue Hole Press, 2010).

Chapter 3

Why Agile Alone May Not Be Enough or the Right Solution, and Why Implementing Agile or Kanban without Good Business Objectives Will Normally Fail

Before digging deep into our new software delivery improvement framework, let's review a case study (inspired from the real world) to see why Agile (including Scrum) may not be enough or the right solution for an IT organization's process needs.

As you will see, it is sometimes a combination of Kanban (Lean) and Agile/Scrum (preliminary case study #1) or Kanban (preliminary case study #2) that will do the trick.

Why Agile Alone May Not Be Enough (Preliminary Case Study #1)

Asia Pacific Services (APS) is a software company offering software development services to companies at a low cost. For many years, APS has been growing, but it has recently encountered competition from several new and larger companies.

Knowing that it will not be able to survive—much less thrive—in this new competitive environment until it improves its software delivery capability, APS management decided to call on a well-known Agile consulting firm to come to its rescue.

Because top management had heard so much about Agile, the vice president in charge of software delivery was asked to implement Agile quickly in his division, an organization of 180 professionals spread throughout Asia.

Initial Planning

The first thing APS management did was to get together with the Agile consultancy to go through an initial planning session. During this session, they had to decide whether to go with a "big bang" implementation or a phased deployment.

After consideration of the pros and cons of the two approaches, the decision was made to deploy Agile using a carefully crafted phased approach to ensure organizational buy-in and to give people and the organization time to mature.

The plan was to first deploy one project team, which would then help train the other three teams.

Pilot Project Team

As part of the plan, APS management quickly selected a team of top professionals to form the first Agile team. They contacted one of their clients who was interested in Agile to include them in their new Agile plan.

They hoped this new quick action would help prevent this client's management from going to the competition and also use this first project team's success to help generate more revenue from both this client and other new clients, using this client as a good reference for their new Agile process.

Initial Project Team Training

Instead of flying everyone to a common location, which may have taken a week or two, it was decided that the people who would be part of this first Agile project would be given a short introduction to Agile via teleconferencing.

Beyond what had been hoped for, the training was a resounding success, with a lot of good feedback.

On-Site Scrum Workshop

Next, an on-site Scrum workshop was offered to the newly assembled Scrum project team in a face-to-face training setting, with the following agenda:

1. Recap of the first Agile training
2. Introduction to Scrum
3. Scrum roles and ceremonies (daily standups, demo, and retrospective, etc.)
4. Scrum in action
    a. Requirements gathering with user stories
    b. User stories estimation and prioritization
    c. Release and iteration planning
5. Technical excellence: test-driven development (TDD), continuous integration, automated testing, etc.
6. Q/A

As had been expected, everyone from the team loved the workshop, considering the information clear and practical. Using their training, they checked on their infrastructure for continuous integration and went immediately into action with their first Sprint planning the following week.

As taught by the Scrum coach, the APS team, with help from the client product owner (PO), were able to quickly identify the user stories, even though they had some questions regarding their level of detail. Nevertheless, they were more interested in getting up and running first, and rightly thought that they could improve the way they write the user stories later on.

Using the new Sprint-based Scrum development cycle, it was decided that the team was to meet with the PO every morning for an hour and go through the details of the user stories together with some of the business users.

With her experience, Joanne Taylor, the coach, insisted that the team and the PO not talk about anything else (as they did when they were still using the waterfall approach) but only about the Scrum user stories.

Another thing she requested from the team was that all developers appear in person, one by one, in front of the business users to work with them on their stories.

To everyone's surprise, this strategy worked out marvelously, and in no time almost all the stories were coded, tested, and declared accepted by the business users who were part of the project team.

Second Sprint: Another Hit for the Team!

Having heard of Agile for a long time, everyone, from the developers to the management team, was delighted that everything went so well also during the second Sprint when they learned that all the users were coded, tested, and approved by the business users as planned (as during the first Sprint).

Third Sprint: Things Started to Rumble

Because things finished so well, APS management decided that they could allow the senior technical lead to leave the project team to take care of some other release work and to help with important presale activity.

This is when the project team realized that they depended heavily on these people for the approval of their design and code, as required by the management team, and this started to generate some dependencies that the team realized Agile or Scrum could not do much about.

Fourth Sprint: Things Became Worse and Worse

As problems never happen in isolation, some of the users started to question what they considered to be missing functionalities, which the technical lead alone could answer. Because the technical lead was not available, some of these users became frustrated and threatened to get in touch with their management to share their concerns.

Fifth Sprint: Project Was Cancelled!

Due to the nature of the overlapping release schedule, which kept the senior technical lead tied up due to some serious problems, the project team was once again late, well behind their schedule with this new Sprint. The team soon learned that the project had been cancelled!

Lessons Learned

By closely assessing the organization's situation and environment, we came to make the following discoveries:

1. Some senior staff members were slow to respond to the team's requests on the new Scrum project because they were multitasking on different releases.
2. There was a lack of knowledge among the team members of the current product architecture, which made all members of the Scrum team depend on the senior technical lead (who had just left the team).
3. The team was still very much used to the command-and-control style and never learned to take initiative or become self-sufficient.
4. There was a lack of communication between the senior technical lead and the rest of the project team (i.e., the project team did not report user concerns about missing functionalities to the senior technical lead).

By taking time to really understand what happened, the management team realized that they were dealing mainly with bottlenecks and dependencies, which Agile or Scrum could not do much about.

After this realization, they made several decisions:

1. As seen in Figure 3.1, the senior technical lead must normally split time between two releases, twelve weeks each, resulting often in delays, unless he works overtime.

    From the lessons learned from this new Scrum project failure, the decision was to shorten the release schedule, from twelve weeks to six weeks, with one following another, as can be seen in Figure 3.2.

    Thanks to this new decision, the senior technical lead is no longer in a multitasking situation, thus allowing him to fully focus on a project at a given point in time.
2. Training and documentation should be initiated immediately to allow the senior technical lead to start training some less senior technical leads to replace him when he is not available.

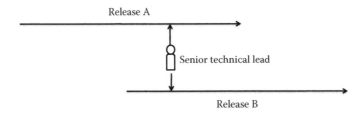

Figure 3.1 Overlapping releases (with multitasking resources).

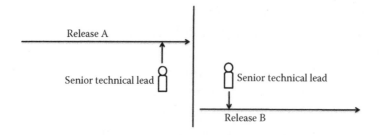

Figure 3.2 Non-overlapping releases (with no multitasking resources).

3. The decision to ask everyone to submit their new code to the senior technical lead is abolished. Instead, the code review should be done by people who are on the project team as part of a peer review, rather than being put in a queue for the senior technical lead alone to review and approve.

From our practice, we have observed very often that a company considers Agile (or Scrum) to be the solution to all their software development problems, whereas, in reality, it may be either Kanban (Lean) or a combination of both Agile and Lean techniques and concepts that are the solution to their organization's needs in terms of process improvement.

The other main lesson learned from this project was that rather than asking the coach to help implement Agile without any assessment, the management team should have asked her to do an assessment of their organization's context and constraints first. This would have allowed them to know what would be best for the organization to implement—perhaps a combination of Agile and Lean techniques rather than just Agile or Scrum alone.

All the previously mentioned reasons are why we have included Kanban (Lean) in this book as part of the potential solution for what the organization would need to improve its software delivery process and capability.

From Scrum to Kanban (Preliminary Case Study #2)

Context

BankCapital is one of the largest retail banks in the world. It has existed more than one hundred years and hopes to serve customers for many more years to come.

Just like any other bank, it has hundreds of applications running on mainframes and a series of newer web applications that, for some, run on their own data. Others have to leverage the service of old RPG mainframe applications to access documentation and financial statements in the back end, which they then deliver to the newer applications to display on the internet for customers to view or to update.

Information Technology

Like many banks, BankCapital invests a lot in technologies, so it should not come as a surprise that it is a big believer in Agile, or more specifically in Scrum, which the bank has rolled out to practically every project team imaginable within their IT department.

There Is Nothing They Do Not Have

Because BankCapital is very successful, money is abundant. Anything they would need to implement Scrum, they have bought for their use, from training time, to tools such as VersionOne or Rally, to coaching time.

Feedback from the Trenches

So, the question now is what can we learn from BankCapital? Plenty, but in particular the fact that Scrum might not be the right solution for their needs, especially for all these back end RPG (report program generator) teams, which had discovered that Scrum was not what they needed but did not have the courage to let top management know.

Finally the Truth Came Out

One day, some of the backend system teams got lucky; a new vice president, who happened to be quite knowledgeable about Agile and Kanban, was brought in to take over their teams.

First, she did not realize that something was wrong with her backend teams, but one day during a conversation with her new teams, she started to realize that whenever she talked about Agile, the only response she got was dead silence.

Surprised by the silence from the team, she pressed on and that is when some of them started to talk. What some of them said was that they never understood why they would need to use Agile, or more specifically Scrum, because working around iterations would not make any sense in their case.

Puzzled, the vice president asked them why. As they went on with their answers, she started to understand and summed all their explanations in these few lines:

No customers or users to interact with
No system to integrate with, except once by the end of the life cycle
No graphical user interface (GUI) to build
Up to ten projects to work on in parallel
Very little new code

Kanban Came to the Rescue

Desiring to be liked by the team, whom she also wanted to help, she organized a meeting the next day to walk them through what she hoped would be the solution to their problems.

First, she agreed with the teams that they should drop the notion of iteration or Sprint because there was no one or no team to test and accept their code delivery by the end of their iteration.

Next, she recommended that they avoid working in parallel on too many projects at the same time, as this has proven to slow teams down. Instead, she suggested that the teams focus on one project at a time, and by doing this she said she was convinced that it would help them speed up their delivery. In addition, she got the team to visualize their workflow and tried to limit their work in progress (WIP), by which notion she meant the number of requests the team could take care of at different stages at a given point in time. By doing this, she said, they would optimize the flow in the same way cities optimize traffic by limiting the number of cars in a lane at a given point in time. The team tried what she said a few days later and started to see that she was right, that working by limiting the WIP resulted in better work flow because there was no congestion on the board.

That was, in summary, how some teams who were applying Scrum within an Agile shop ended up making the move to Kanban.

Pitfalls of New Software Processes (Preliminary Case Study #3)

A while back when business was still booming, it was good to work at Food Service Software (FSS), a software provider in the grocery space with about 350 IT professionals.

But one of their clients, the Central Market (CM), was not completely happy with FSS's software delivery and quality. As CM management heard about Agile, they asked to meet with Mark Hudd, FSS's vice president of software development, to ask FSS to implement Agile.

Given the fact that CM was a very important client (it would be catastrophic to lose CM as a client), Mark readily agreed to implement Agile, and especially Scrum, to improve FSS's customer satisfaction.

As soon as Mark and some of his senior team members came back from a meeting with CM management, he immediately decided to call an Agile service provider to schedule some Scrum training for his development staff.

As soon as the team finished their training, Mark met with them to talk about the new piece of software that CM management wanted the team to start working on as part of their new strategic direction for the new year.

As soon as the FSS team got together the following Monday, you could sense the enthusiasm in the air. The team talked highly about their Agile, and especially Scrum, training and how much they had learned.

Eager to move forward, Mary Beth, the FSS team's ScrumMaster, suggested that they should immediately contact John Dean, CM's vice president of software technology. They wanted him to appoint a PO for the new project who would be responsible for providing the FSS team with a clear vision and direction for the new project.

As the person behind the request that FSS move into Scrum, John Dean was glad to let the team know that Andrew Kosko had received his PO training and was available to meet the next morning to start working on this new project.

Release and Sprint Planning

Excitement was in the air the following morning when the FSS project team met with Andrew Kosko. Even if Andrew was relatively new to CM, he was quite knowledgeable and was able to quickly identify some main user stories for the team to start working on.

This is not to say that there was not some difficulty. But Andrew was able to contact some of the senior staff back at his office to answer some of the team's questions during the requirements gathering workshop.

Prioritizing the user stories together as a team, they were able to divide them around four Sprints, each with nine or ten stories for the team to work on during a three-week schedule.

Scrum Ceremonies

Like Andrew, Mary Beth was also excited and wanted to show the team how much she could contribute. Serving as the team's ScrumMaster, she spent the weekend prior to the meeting drafting some guidelines about the different meeting types, called ceremonies, to adapt Scrum to their environment.

The way Mary Beth saw it, there were two types of meetings they should hold.

First, there is a series of meetings in the morning called Daily Standups where all the team members were asked to come together to get synchronized to know how much closer they are to the Sprint goal. To do this, Mary Beth suggested that the team members answer three well-known questions:

1. What did you do yesterday?
2. What do you plan on doing today?
3. Are there any obstacles in your way?

In addition to this morning meeting, there was a second type of daily meeting in the afternoon, which Mary Beth saw essentially as a working session with Andrew Kosko, the PO, and some business users.

First Month

Everything went well during the first month and after the demo, Andrew Kosko, the PO, sent the FSS team an e-mail to let them know that all of the user stories that were part of the first iteration had been approved. Management, as well as the team, were so excited. After three long weeks of work, they had now moved from spectators to Agile actors. How exciting!

Change in Product Owner

Business life would be quite smooth if there were no change, but this was not the case with CM. As Mary Beth just had learned, some changes took place with the arrival of Rich Desmond, a new vice president who had just arrived. But Rich Desmond did not arrive alone—he brought with him a friend, Jesse Wang, whom he trusts completely, to ask him to serve as the new PO for the project.

Different Understanding of Agile and Scrum

With the arrival of the new PO, the team came to realize, after a few days discussion about what to do with the iteration bugs, that not everyone had the same understanding about Agile and Scrum.

Because Jesse was new to CM business, Rich asked Helen Tong, a long-time business manager with CM, to team up with him to also serve as PO to help Jesse move the project forward. The FSS team was concerned and objected that there should be only one PO, but FSS insisted that Jesse and Helen both serve as POs while Jesse Wang was still new to FSS.

Maybe because they had to give in to the demand of CM that both Helen and Jesse serve as POs that the FSS team took this opportunity to raise the question that not all bugs will be fixed during the iteration. This, they said, will help move the project ahead until the system integration testing phase where all the project bugs will be taken care of. Even though Jesse was still new, he was in disagreement with FSS's proposal and insisted that all bugs be fixed before the team moved to the next iteration. So, it was decided.

Building New Expectations

As the next week started, the team got together with the two POs to get going anew. Jesse let the team know that he had been given a new budget envelope and raised the question of how long and how much it would take FSS to build this new piece of software for whatever work remained. One of the FSS team members explained that in Agile, there is no way that they would know how much and how long it will take the team to build the software ahead of time like in Waterfall. Hearing this, Jesse retorted that Agile or not, he would need, per management's request, to know how much it was going to cost CM and how quickly they could hope to see this piece of software released in operations.

The discussion went back and forth and the two sides were at an impasse. It was then that Mark Honke, the most senior FSS team lead, stood up and said he had an idea that could lead to the solution for the problem CM raised. He suggested the two sides meet together to go through the list of all the user stories and come up with an agreement as to what was expected from each one of them. Everyone agreed.

Later that week, a meeting was called where they went through the list of all the user stories with some newly invited business users, all trying to understand what CM business people would expect from each story to determine what they would agree to in terms of design and functionality.

The atmosphere was rather nice and everyone was in good mood. So, the two-day meeting went by very fast.

The following week, one of the business analysts from the CM side sent out the list of all the user stories along with the notes he had taken for the CM side to review and approve. But one week went by without any word from the CM side. It was then that FSS's most senior team member suggested that "silence equals approval" and therefore told the rest of the FSS team that they should make the assumption that the two sides were in agreement. This is how FSS started to use the newly created design notes as the basis for their new development.

Nice Surprise

To everyone's surprise on the FSS side, the two POs complemented one another well by making all the decisions together. Because Jesse was new, one could have expected that sometimes he would have to get in touch with senior business managers for advice before he could make a business decision for the project, but with Helen's presence, Jesse's questions got answered very quickly by Helen. Things went so well between the two POs that the team was soon done with Sprint #2 with all the user stories once again approved.

Agile Started to Rumble

Only with Sprint #3 did something start to go astray. Some of the CM business users began to ask questions about why such and such a story did not produce the functionality expected.

The answer invariably given was that this is what they had agreed to during the design meeting, as had been noted in the design notes they had sent to the CM side.

It was then that Helen said that they never understood that they had to approve the design notes because, for them, they were only a few notes that were taken informally, rather than a contractual agreement between the two sides.

On and on the discussion went. In the end, this became almost an untenable situation for the FSS team to be in, which ended up turning the previously good relationship into a mistrusting one, which, in turn, ended up spoiling the whole working atmosphere.

Back to Waterfall and Command and Control

It was then that the CM team said that they would either cancel the project or have the FSS team go back to work using the previous CM process with all the software gatings/control milestones.

Given the bad economy and their desire to satisfy the customer at any cost, the FSS team acquiesced and moved back to using the CM's process, which was mainly a waterfall approach with some heavy need for documentation and reporting.

Six months later, the project was still not done. With every week came a new request and complaint from CM as to how slow the FSS team was, just like before. The FSS team went from paradise to hell, some of the team members said privately.

BUSINESS GOALS– DRIVEN IT-WIDE SOFTWARE DELIVERY IMPROVEMENT FRAMEWORK

II

We hope that if you read our book up to here, it would become obvious to you that Agile alone is not a panacea for everything. The same thing should be true of Kanban (and Lean), which, sometimes, may be best combined with Agile (or Scrum) to form a powerful solution to an organization's needs.

Likewise, we hope that you have seen that implementing new processes with soft objectives alone will also lead to failure, as demonstrated in preliminary case study #3.

This is what has led us to come up with the business-driven process improvement framework, as described in this book, which, in our mind, can serve as a generic approach for a software delivery improvement program, whether the process you are looking at is Agile (XP and Scrum), Kanban (Lean), or a combination of the two.

11

BUSINESS GOALS-DRIVEN IT-WIDE SOFTWARE DELIVERY IMPROVEMENT FRAMEWORK

Chapter 4

Seven-Step Software Delivery Improvement Framework

Unlike some of those fervent Agile proponents who think the Agile process is "the end all and be all" solution of our IT ills, our approach to IT process improvement is based not on some vague process improvement for the sake of process, but on an organization's business needs and goals—the only condition for any process improvement effort to have a measurable and lasting success (see Figure 4.1).

Description

Step 1: Identify the Business Sponsor and Her or His Needs and Goals

As long as we recognize that the main objective in building software is to support a business, it will become obvious that for a software delivery improvement program to be successful, we have to link it to some specific business goals. This is the reason why the first step is to identify the owner of these business goals for whom you are supposed to implement this IT improvement effort.

Identify the Business Sponsor

Knowing whose business goals this IT effort is supposed to help achieve will help you identify the goals that will drive your improvement effort, as well as determine the metrics you should use to measure your achievement.

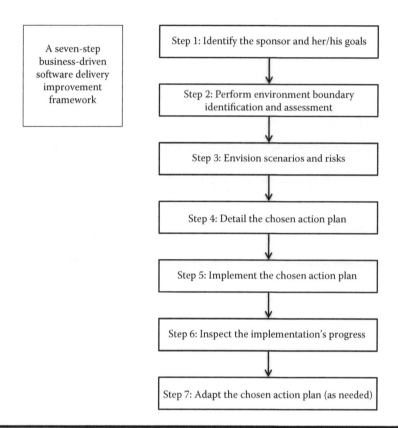

Figure 4.1   A seven-step software delivery improvement framework.

Identify Business Problems and Issues

Whether the idea to improve software delivery capability comes from within IT or from the business, it will always address some business problems and issues, which the business sponsor tries to solve.

For illustration purposes, examples of problems or issues that have to be corrected can be one of the following:

■ Complaint that software delivered does not meet requirements, to better serve the company's customers
■ Complaint that the software delivered contains a very high number of bugs, which make the customers' experience very unpleasant
■ Complaint that it takes too long to deliver software while the competitor usually brings out new software in half the time

Identifying specific problems like these will help identify business goals and their measurements that help lead the IT improvement effort, which we address later.

Identify Business and IT Goals

We will delve into more details later, but here we provide some examples of business goals from which we can deduct the IT goals for the improvement effort.

1. Business goal:
   - Increase the number of customers who visit our website by 5%.

   IT goals:
   - It should take the customers less than 1 minute to register their information.
   - The number of bugs should be reduced by 50%.
2. Business goal:
   - Increase the number of newly registered customers by 3% every quarter.

   IT goals:
   - Project deadline should be reduced by 10%.
   - Key features should be delivered 10% times faster.

Identify Measurements

From the previous list of goals, we can identify the following as their respective measurements:

- Number of unused features by users
- Variance in delivery timeline

Step 2: Perform Environment Boundary Identification and Assessment

Even though the title of this book mentions IT-wide improvement, this does not mean that the whole IT department is going to be the object of an immediate and big-bang rollout. Rather, what we have seen work in the majority of cases is a phased implementation strategy that progressively takes the IT organization from an unsuccessful situation to a controlled state where the IT project is well undertaken and delivered. For this, what you will need to do first is to identify the boundary of organization that will be impacted by this IT-wide implementation.

Identify the Boundary

To do this, first meet and ask your business sponsor for the environment under her or his direction that will be the target of this IT improvement effort.

Environment Assessment

After identifying the boundary, contact everyone who will be impacted by the improvement effort, on both the business and the IT side, to find out what they think about the current situation and to gather suggestions and ideas that could help facilitate their buy-in for the success of this IT implementation effort.

Findings Summary

Because the result of the assessment could be lengthy, you are advised to sum up the findings in some sort of executive summary. Doing this will help facilitate both the discussion with the executive sponsor(s) and your own vision of what the future solution should address, in terms of key improvements from the current environment.

Step 3: Envision Scenarios and Risks

Before selecting one (best) improvement plan, experience has led us to believe that having two or three scenarios (options) is always something we would like to first come up with. Not only does this give top management and some key leaders an opportunity to see which scenario will address most of their needs, but it also provides them with an opportunity to provide input. This will, then, in turn allow them to take ownership of the solution as theirs and not that of an outsider.

In building these scenarios (options), please also remember to identify all the risks that are associated with each one of them. You should carefully point them out to the management team to ensure that they are fully aware of their impact on the future implementation.

Step 4: Detail the Chosen Action Plan

Once management and some of the key leaders have had the opporutnity to go through the pros and cons of the various scenarios (options), ask them to chose one of these scenarios or a combination of them to create a single plan from which to implement the improvement effort.

Step 5: Implement the Chosen Action Plan

Once the plan has been detailed and presented back to the management team for review, it is time to get prepared for execution.

Depending on what section of the business will be impacted by the chosen plan, the composition of the steering committee to follow up on the execution will be essential. The key thing is to make sure that the committee has access to up-to-date and accurate information for their understanding and help with removing impediments.

As the late management guru Peter Drucker often said, "Strategy is execution." What this means, in our case, is that having a plan is a good first step, but knowing how to execute it is what counts the most.

Step 6: Inspect the Implementation's Progress

As the popular saying goes, "A plan is only a plan." This is to say that we should expect some deviation from the chosen plan when it comes time to execute it. This is also to say that it is key to continuously inspect the execution's progress and remove impediments to help keep it moving.

Step 7: Adapt the Chosen Action Plan (as Needed)

While inspecting the plan's progress, you may need to make adaptations to the plan to make adjustments to the changes in the organization and surrounding business environment, depending on the level and nature of their impacts.

Summary

This chapter introduced some of the reasons why most companies fail in scaling Agile or Lean at the IT-wide level. To prevent this from happening to future implementation, we also presented a seven-step process improvement framework, which is based on the company's business needs and goals.

Chapter 5

Step 1: Identify the (Business) Sponsor and Her or His Needs and Goals

If you have been asked to improve software delivery for the whole IT department or the whole enterprise all at once, your sponsor will likely be the CIO or CEO. If you have been asked to improve IT capability for only a specific business or IT unit, even a very large one, then your sponsor will be someone else, whom you will need to get to know very quickly.

Before we delve into the sponsor's needs, let's explain why we have put the term *business* in parentheses before *sponsor*. The reason for this is because even if the main unit in charge of this process improvement is some unit within the IT department, it is very often some unit on the business side that is at the origin of this need for IT to improve its capability.

Identify the (Business) Sponsor(s)

Identifying the sponsor is, as we have said before, one of the most important things you will do because she or he is the one who will let you know if what you do is in line with her or his goals.

So, the question now is how do we know who the business sponsor of the improvement effort is? A quick answer to this question is whoever is responsible for the final funding of this initiative, even if the IT budget could be used, in the first place, to pay for this effort. So, for instance, if the IT unit plans on charging the expense back to the marketing department, then the marketing executive will be the business sponsor for this effort. This being said, because IT is the first spender for this initiative, the IT director or executive in charge of marketing will become the other sponsor of this IT effort. This is why we add an *s* in parentheses following the word *sponsor*; that is, to indicate the fact that the sponsor may be more than one.

Identify the Sponsor(s)' Needs and Goals

Once you know the business or IT sponsor(s) for this initiative, the next step is to plan a meeting to identify her or his needs and goals.

Based on our experience, we recommend you put together a list of questions, such as the ones in Figures 5.1 and 5.2, to help facilitate information gathering. Given these executives' or leaders' busy schedule, we recommend that you send this list to them at least three or four days before the meeting, to allow them enough time to review and answer questions for the interview.

The type of questionnaire or questions will vary somewhat depending on whether your sponsor(s) is (are) from IT or a business leader from the business.

Although most of the questions are self-explanatory, we suggest that you explain to the executives that the goals follow the SMART rule; that is, any goal should be specific, measurable, achievable, and realistic within a reasonable time frame (SMART).

---

1. What do you consider to be the five most important items for your business unit?
2. What do you consider to be the five most important items for your business unit in working with IT?
3. What are your business goals in general?
4. What are the five most important goals for you in dealing with IT, and especially with IT in software development and maintenance?
5. What are IT's biggest weaknesses in supporting your business goals?
6. How do you think IT is most effective in helping you achieve your goals?
7. What is the timeline you would like to see for this IT improvement effort?

Figure 5.1   Example of business needs and goals questionnaire.

---

1. What do you consider to be the five most important items for your unit?
2. What do you consider to be the five most important items for your unit in working with the business?
3. What are your top five goals?
4. What are the five most important goals for you in dealing with the business, and especially with regard to software development and maintenance?
5. From what you know, what are IT's biggest weaknesses in supporting the business goals?
6. In what areas is IT most effective in helping the business achieve their goals?
7. What is the timeline you would like to see for this IT improvement effort?

Figure 5.2 Example of questionnaire and questions for IT sponsors.

Under the SMART rule, goals such as "customer satisfaction" or "increased performance" will not make the cut because they are neither specific nor measurable, and neither achievable nor realistic within a reasonable time frame.

By contrast, goals such as "reducing the number of software bugs by 5% with the third release" or "increasing the number of delivered features by 10% within three months" are quite acceptable.

Because one of the main strengths of our approach is the linkage between goals and solution items, we will be using the cause-and-effect diagramming technique, also called the fishbone diagram, to identify not only the goals and their sub-goals but also the corresponding action items.

To illustrate how to use this cause-and-effect diagramming technique, let's assume that we have identified one of the main IT goals ("Reduce software bugs by 4% with the next release") along with two sub-goals ("Double the number of testing time by twice the current amount" and "Double the number of written test cases to be applied"). Figures 5.3 and 5.4 show how these goals can be represented using the fishbone diagramming technique.

1. Reduce software
   bugs by 4% with the
   next release

Figure 5.3 The first goal.

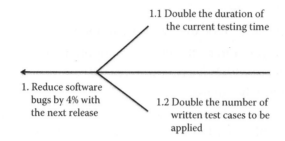

Figure 5.4   The first goal with its two sub-goals.

Business Areas	Goals	Measurements
1. Business development	Increase profit by 5% by year end	Revenue variance
2. Customer service	Reduce new project bugs by 20%	Number of bugs and number of customer calls about bug issues
	Reduce the time to resolve a complaint by 10% of the current time	The time spent over the phone with the customer

Figure 5.5   Goals and measurements by business area.

Having identified some precise goals, the next thing you will need to do is to identify their measurement. Figure 5.5 provides an example of the types of measures that can be used to support some of the goals that were identified.

Summary

This chapter introduced the reader to the concepts and examples of goals and their measurements.

Chapter 6

Step 2: Perform Environment Boundary Identification and Assessment

Knowing the business sponsor will not only help uncover the sponsor's goals but also identify the environment boundary for what should be accomplished. Depending on who the sponsor is, the environment—and its boundary—to assess will vary.

How to Identify the Environment Boundary

To identify the environment boundary, first ask for an organizational chart of the unit under that business and IT executive's leadership and responsibility. Next, you may want to meet with that executive to ask her or him which units of the organization are within the limits of this process improvement effort.

Figure 6.1 is an example of an organizational structure under the concerned executive. From Figure 6.1, we can deduce that the organization to be assessed will look like the one in Figure 6.2.

Another example of a business sponsor can be found in Figure 6.3. As a consequence, the environment to be assessed will be similar to that shown in Figure 6.4. From Figure 6.4, we can deduce the IT organization that is in charge of this sponsor's business units, which can look somewhat like Figure 6.5.

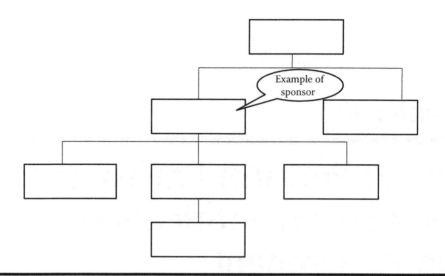

Figure 6.1 One example of a business sponsor.

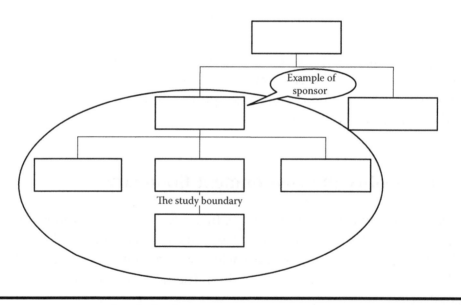

Figure 6.2 One example of a business sponsor.

Assess the Identified Business and IT Environment

Once the environment boundary has been identified for both the business side and the IT side, the assessment of this environment should be done as soon as possible. To this effect, Figures 6.6 and 6.7 list the types of questions to ask different members of this environment.

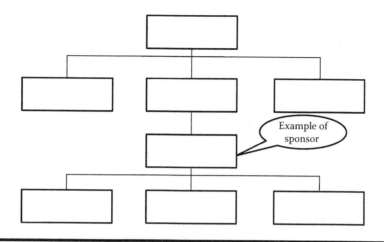

Figure 6.3   Another business sponsor, at a lower level.

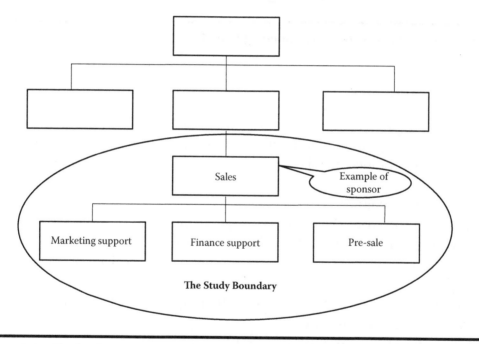

Figure 6.4   The business sponsor's boundary.

Depending on whether it is the business unit or the IT team you want to assess, the type of questionnaire or questions will vary, whether it is for the business side (Figure 6.6) or the IT side (Figure 6.7).

Figure 6.8 is an example of the types of answers we got from having submitted the assessment questionnaire to IT (i.e., the assessment questionnaire shown in Figure 6.7).

Figure 6.5   Identifying the corresponding IT unit.

Findings Summary

With so many questions and so many answers, especially for a large organization, it is helpful to sum them up into easy-to-understand and easy-to-remember key points, as follows:

1. Specialists' culture
2. Most of the work done for very large clients
3. A lack of interaction with the business client
4. Some unhappiness about the team estimate (due to lack of good decomposition)
5. Client somewhat concerned about the number of tickets being taken care of for every release
6. A strong architectural background

Summary

This chapter introduced the concept of environment boundary and how to identify it. It next introduced a questionnaire sample that can be used to assess the strengths and weaknesses of the environment.

Agile and Lean Enterprise Implementation Assessment Questionnaire

Organization

1. Describe the organization under your direction.
2. How do you interact with the business or IT on a project?
3. Do you have all the resources needed to carry out a project? Please describe.
4. What are the strongest points of your team?
5. What are the weakest points of your team?
6. Have you ever received any criticism or praise from the business for your team? Please describe.
7. What would you do to improve the collaboration with IT/business?
8. How would you restructure the organization if you were given the opportunity to do so?

Development Infrastructure

1. Please describe your software development and maintenance infrastructure.
2. What are your infrastructure's strongest points?
3. What are your infrastructure's weakest points?
4. What is your plan to improve your infrastructure? Please describe.
5. What have been the biggest problems with your infrastructure?
6. What has been the biggest praise for your infrastructure?
7. What team is responsible for infrastructure and how is it organized?
8. How would you restructure the infrastructure if you were given the opportunity to do so?

Team

1. How is the team under your direction organized?
2. How do your team members work together on a project or on a maintenance request?
3. How familiar is your team with Agile concepts?
4. How familiar is your team with Lean concepts?
5. Which people know Agile the best?
6. Which people know Lean concepts the best?
7. Is there anyone you would consider to be a potential problem?
8. How would you restructure the team if you were given the opportunity to do so?

Figure 6.6   Example of satisfaction assessment questionnaire and questions for the IT side.

Agile and Lean Enterprise Implementation Assessment Questionnaire

Technology and Application

1. What is your development technology stack? Please describe.
2. Is there any change in plans? Please describe.
3. What has been the weakest point of your technology stack?
4. What has been considered the strongest point of your technology stack?
5. What does your team know the most about this technology stack?
6. What does your team know the least about this technology stack?
7. Is your application architecture visible and/or fully documented?
8. What would you do to improve this technology stack if you were given the opportunity to do so?

IT Process

1. What is your current IT software process for development?
2. What is your current IT software process for maintenance?
3. Who represents what areas in this process? Please describe.
4. What are the strongest points of your development process?
5. What are the strongest points of your maintenance process?
6. What are the weakest points of your development process?
7. What are the weakest points of your maintenance process?
8. How would you improve the development and maintenance processes if you were given the opportunity to do so?

The Business

1. How is (are) the business unit(s) you work with organized?
2. What do they normally need from your IT team?
3. In what areas have they been the most appreciative of your team? Please describe.
4. In what areas have they been the most negative of your team? Please describe.
5. Whom from the business unit(s) has your team interacted with the most?
6. How would you qualify that interaction? Negative? Positive?
7. How would you qualify the level of knowledge of the business unit(s)?
8. What changes would you make to the business unit(s) to make your working with them even more effective? Please describe.

Figure 6.6 (continued)   Example of satisfaction assessment questionnaire and questions for the IT side.

Organization

1. Describe the business organization under your direction or which you are part of.
2. How do you interact with IT on a project?
3. Do you have all the resources needed to carry out a project? Please describe.
4. What are the strongest points of your team in your interaction with IT?
5. What are the weakest points of your team in your interaction with IT?
6. Have you ever received any criticism or praise from IT for your team? Please describe.
7. What would you do to improve the collaboration with IT?
8. How would you restructure the organization if you were given the opportunity to do so?

Team

1. How is the team under your direction organized?
2. How do your team members work together with IT on a project or on a maintenance request?
3. How familiar is your team with Agile concepts?
4. How familiar is your team with Lean concepts?
5. Which people know Agile the best?
6. Which people know Lean concepts the best?
7. Is there anyone you would consider to be a potential problem?
8. How would you restructure the team if you were given the opportunity to do so?

IT Process

1. What do you know about the current IT software process for development?
2. What do you know about the current IT software process for maintenance?
3. Who represents your area in working with IT?
4. What are the strongest points of the IT development process?
5. What are the strongest points of the IT maintenance process?
6. What are the weakest points of the IT development process?
7. What are the weakest points of the IT maintenance process?
8. How would you like to improve the IT development and maintenance processes if you were given you the opportunity to do so?

Figure 6.7   Example of assessment questionnaire and questions for the business side.

IT Organization

1. How is (are) the IT unit(s) you work with organized?

2. What do they normally need from your team?

3. In what areas have you been the most appreciative of their team? Please describe.

4. In what areas have you been the most negative of their team? Please describe.

5. Whom from the IT unit(s) has your team interacted with the most?

6. How would you qualify that interaction? Negative? Positive?

7. How would you qualify the level of knowledge of the IT unit(s)?

8. What changes would you make to the IT unit(s) to make your working with them even more effective? Please describe.

Figure 6.7 (continued)   Example of assessment questionnaire and questions for the business side.

Organization

1. An organization based on the specialists' culture
2. Teams organized by technical specialties
3. Project team size varies from project to project
4. Lack of a dedicated QA team

Development Infrastructure

1. A good infrastructure at least in terms of software integration
2. Lack of a good servers cluster that sometimes leads to system crashes
3. No automated testing foundation

Team Knowledge

1. Good team knowledge about software architecture
2. Good architectural documentation
3. Lack of cross-training between functional teams

Technology and Application

1. Old technology stack
2. Need to upgrade the current technology

Process

1. Waterfall
2. Many reviews
3. Very strict project management
4. Lack of a formal testing process
5. Lack of a good way to estimate our projects
6. Lack of user participation

Business

1. Clients' business users seem to follow their own process, which is not the same as ours
2. Not all business users are knowledgeable about their area, perhaps due to some turnover on their side
3. Lack of user time for acceptance testing
4. User requirements are not always clearly written
5. Have expressed concerns about our team's throughput

Figure 6.8   Examples of summarized answers to the assessment questionnaire shown in Figure 6.7.

Step 3: Envision Scenarios and Risks

Rather than coming up with only one single solution right away, experience has led us to believe that it will be much more effective for the organization's buy-in if some high-level scenarios (options) can be proposed for the management and leadership team to look at first.

In addition to the psychological buy-in, this will allow top management and key leaders to provide their feedback, which will give the chosen solution a better chance to be successful.

The logic behind this idea is the same, for instance, as when someone wants to take a trip to go from one city to another (as in Figure 7.1). Maybe itinerary #1 is the shortest way to get from city A to city B, but what if its roads are full of roadblocks? What if itinerary #2 is a little bit longer, but its roads are safer and smoother to drive on? From this analogy, you can see why it is preferable to come up with different scenarios for management and the leadership to review first and to choose the final solution from.

From Goals to Action Items (in Bypassing the Assessment)

Now that we are convinced that we should come up with some scenarios first, the question is how to come up with the different action items (and scenarios).

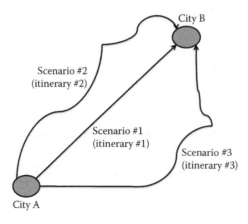

Figure 7.1 What is the best itinerary (scenario) to get from city A to city B?

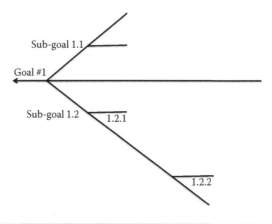

Figure 7.2 From goals to sub-goals.

To answer this question, let's go back to the fishbone diagramming technique and the goals that had been previously identified in Chapter 5, as can be seen in Figure 7.2.

From Figure 7.2, we can identify, using the same cause-and-effect technique, all the action items needed for all the goals and sub-goals (as in Figure 7.3).

By the end of the exercise, we can use a table to centralize all the action items for all the goals and sub-goals, dimension by dimension (Figure 7.4).

Or, we can also organize the result of the brainstorming by goals and sub-goals, as in Figure 7.5.

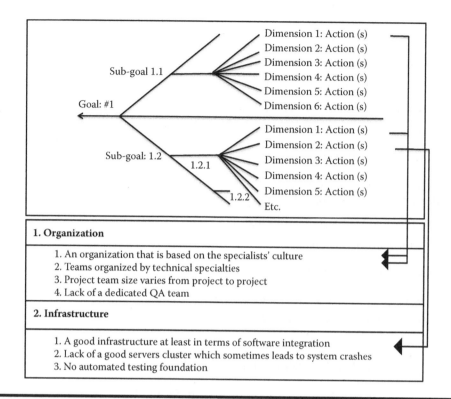

Figure 7.3 **From all goals and sub-goals to all action items.**

How to Identify Risks (for Different Scenarios)

Even with the table represented in Figure 7.5, the work is far from finished; you still have to identify all the associated risks for a more thorough evaluation.

Risk identification is a serious and broad subject in itself, but for this book's purpose, we will limit ourselves only to some of its most visible aspects, especially for the type of subject we talk about in this book.

To this effect, ask yourself, for every action item of the solutions, "What if something goes wrong with this or that item of this or that scenario? What about its impact, ranking, and probability that it may happen?"

Some examples of how things could go wrong:

1. What if the architectural documentation isn't done on time?
2. What if the automatic testing infrastructure isn't in place before integration testing starts?

By the end of this exercise, do not forget to create a table to recapitalize (Figure 7.6).

Organization (Dimension)

1. Keep the specialist's culture.
2. Reorganize the team by product line architecture.
3. Keep team size at around twelve people.
4. Hire more QA personnel specialized in automated testing.

Infrastructure (Dimension)

1. Set up a new development and support infrastructure, at least in terms of continuous integration, automated testing.
2. Reinforce development server clusters.
3. Build automated test cases.

Team Knowledge (Dimension)

1. Spread team knowledge about architecture.
2. Create architectural documentation.
3. Cross-train.

Technology and Application (Dimension)

1. Make the architecture more visible by documenting it.
2. Keep the current technology.

Process (Dimension)

1. Use a combination of Agile and Kanban.
2. Combine the first two phases into one (Requirements/Analysis Design and Coding).
3. Create a process lead role.
4. Incorporate user acceptance testing into the process.
5. There will be no demo like in Agile or Scrum.
6. The product owner will not be part of the team but represent the client outside of the team.
7. The development will have actual business users embedded into their teams.

Business (Dimension)

1. Train the clients' business users to the process.
2. Require that they be available throughout the project life cycle.

Figure 7.4 Action items for all the goals and sub-goals, organized by dimension.

Goals	Sub-goals	Action Items (Organized around the Six Dimensions)	Sub-action Items (Optional)
#1	#1.1	Organization: 1.1.a. Keep the specialist's culture. 1.1.b. Reorganize the team by product line. 1.1.c. Keep team size at around twelve. 1.1.d. Hire more QA team specialized in automated testing. Infrastructure: 1.1.a. etc. 1.2.b. etc. Etc.	
	#1.2		

Figure 7.5 **Another example of action items for all the goals and sub-goals, organized by dimension.**

Goals	Sub-goals	Action Items	Sub-action Items	Risk	Impact	Mitigation Plan

Figure 7.6 **A recapitalization table.**

Scenario Consolidation

In reviewing the previous action items, you will see that some of them are the same for some goals or sub-goals, which you will be, then, required to consolidate or merge.

Next, using the answers from the assessment as the reference, you will try to create the first scenario (scenario #1), which should contain the best answers to the most goals and sub-goals as possible (see Figures 7.7, 7.8, and 7.9).

To these scenarios, remember to add some indication as to the implementation timeline, resource needs, and associated costs.

Scenario #1	Goals	Sub-goals	Action Items	Sub-action Items	Risk	Impact	Mitigation Plan

Figure 7.7   Scenario #1.

Scenario #2	Goals	Sub-goals	Action Items	Sub-action Items	Risk	Impact	Mitigation Plan

Figure 7.8   Scenario #2.

Scenario #3	Goals	Sub-goals	Action Items	Sub-action Items	Risk	Impact	Mitigation Plan

Figure 7.9   Scenario #3.

Scenarios

Scenarios	Action Items	Sub-action Items	Risks/Impact	Mitigation
Scenario #1	(organized by tracks…)			
Scenario #2	(organized by tracks…)			
Scenario #3	(organized by tracks…)			

Figure 7.10   A summary of all the scenarios.

Depending on the size of the implementation effort, do not forget to create some type of summarized table, as can be seen in Figure 7.10, to give the leadership and management an overall view without becoming lost in the details.

Summary

This chapter discussed the need to envision various scenarios of associated risks for management to review and select the best fit for the environment.

Chapter 8

Step 4: Detail the Chosen Action Plan

Once a scenario, or combination of items from different scenarios, has been selected, the next step is to develop the details needed for its execution.

For the organization's buy-in, it is important that all respected players be involved in the elaboration of this chosen action plan.

Anatomy of a Detailed Scenario (Chosen Action Plan)

The first thing to do is to develop the plan along the different tracks of the assessment, which are to support the different business goals that had been identified. The other reason to create a multi-thronged plan with a few tracks to be led by some of the key players is not only to get the buy-in from the leaders, but also to create some belief for others to follow them.

Next you should identify items that will become the "requisites" for the overall solution (Figure 8.1):

A. Common action items
   1. Organizational
     a. Leave most of the current teams alone (as they are already busy billing), while building a new team with people borrowed from the first Agile team to better infuse new blood and show the new way—Option 1.

Detailed Action Plan

	Goals	Measurements	Action Items	Dependencies
A. Common action items 　1. Organizational 　2. Technical				
B. Action Tracks 　1. Track #1 　　a. Action item 　　b. Action item 　　c. Action item 　2. Track #2 　　a. Action item 　　b. Action item 　3. Track #3				
C. Timeline				
D. Budget 　1. Hiring 　2. Training				

Figure 8.1　Anatomy of a detailed plan.

　　　b. The same as above with QA (quality assurance) team's reporting to Operations—Option 2.
　　　c. Hire around ten more people with the right skills and organization in order to show the way with fewer disturbances to the current billing operations while also positioning us for the future business development—Option 3.
　　2. Technical
　　　a. Organize training to team to architecture
　　　b. Visibility into the application architecture (black box)
　　　c. Training to both application and domain knowledge
　　　d. Application and standard documentation
　B. Action tracks (see Figure 8.2)

Action items	Management Track (#1)	Internal Track					Customer Track (#7)
		Release Planning Track (#2)	Infrastructure Track (#3)	Organization Track (#4)	Wastes and Bottlenecks Track (#5)	Production Support Track (#6)	
		·					

Figure 8.2   Action tracks.

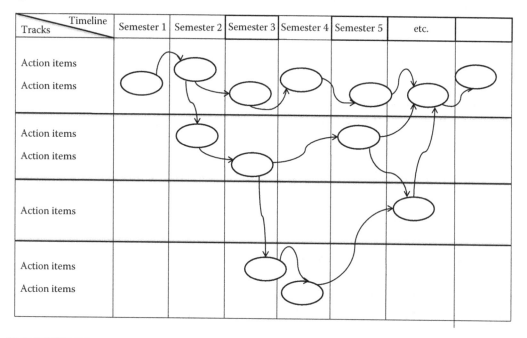

Figure 8.3   Timeline for the action plan.

C. Timeline

The next thing to do is to put the action plan into a timeline, as can be seen in Figure 8.3.

D. Budget

Next, to determine how much money will be needed to implement this plan, remember to total up all the capital expenditures and expenses

Capital
Capital budget purchases
• Action item #1
• Action item #2
Future Initiatives
• Action item #1
• Action item #2
Expenses
Operations
Application and Development
• Action item #1
• Action item #2
Maintenance
• Action item #1
Grand total

Figure 8.4 Budget for the action plan.

that will be required for this implementation into a budget, more or less as in Figure 8.4.

Seven Characteristics of a Good Action Plan

As a reminder of what you should do to be successful with your action plan, make sure that it has the following seven characteristics, as seen in Figure 8.5:

1. Clear business goals (which the plan is intended to support)
2. Logical and easy to understand
   Given the numerous times we have seen sophisticated plans fail, make sure that your plan is logical and easy to understand. Simplicity is key.
3. Organized around small chunks of achievable results

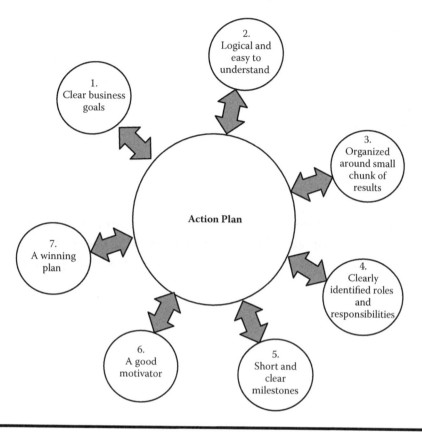

Figure 8.5 The seven characteristics of a good action plan.

Even if the plan may last a year or two, it is critical to organize the work around small chunks of work that can be achieved in a fairly short time frame.

4. Clearly identified roles and responsibilities

To obtain people's buy-in and confidence that the plan will be successful, it is critical to get the key people involved. By key people, we do not necessarily mean managerial people, but people who are respected and trusted and clearly identify the roles they will play in the improvement plan.

5. Short and clear milestones

The reason why we recommend you to identify clear and short milestones is to ensure that the organization has some opportunity to celebrate their intermediate successes, especially to keep the momentum going.

6. A good motivator
   You should ensure that the plan is an opportunity to provide some motivation, rather than fear to the teams. An example of this will be to show that if the plan is successfully executed, then everyone will have a more meaningful work environment.
7. A winning plan

Summary

This chapter presented details of the so-called action plan. It not only showed how to develop one, but also how to build a budget for it. Likewise, it serves as a reminder of the seven qualities of a good action plan.

Chapter 9

Step 5: Implement the Chosen Action Plan

It is good to have a vision and even better to have a plan on paper. This being said, it is, as the late management guru Peter Drucker used to say, a skillful execution makes all the difference.

Set Up the Implementation Structure

Depending on the organization and its context, there are many ways to organize an effective execution of the chosen plan. From our experience, it is fundamental to create a steering committee (or governing committee, as one managing director we used to advise called it) and a coordination group who will be responsible for the reporting of the execution progress to the steering committee (as seen in Figure 9.1).

Like many things in life, when it comes to real-life execution, you can be sure that not everything will go smoothly. From our experience, the best known causes of failures for process improvement come from three things:

1. Lack of commitment from management
   Even if your action plan looks good, your team members will eventually see that you are not fully committed to go through the process if you switch or let people switch back and forth between the old and new process and/or between the old and new management style.

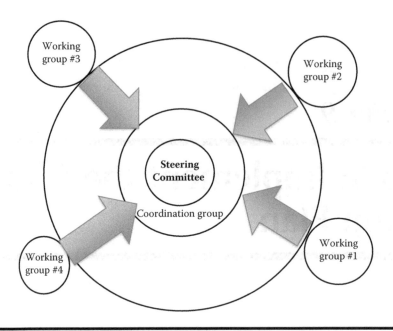

Figure 9.1 Implementation—Organization.

In other words, they will perceive you as "not walking your walk or talking your talk."

2. Lack of available resources

There may be nothing worse than not making resources available for the implementation but this is unfortunately what we see too often in too many cases.

3. Resistance to change

Resistance to change is almost as human as change itself, as long as people are not sure about the impact of this change on their life or career. So, make sure to remember to communicate a winning message to everyone as often as needed. If you take enough precaution to make sure that your plan execution does not lack in these areas, you will likely succeed.

Seven Characteristics of an Effective Plan Execution

In the same vein as the seven points to remember for a good action plan, the following are a set of seven points you may want to keep in mind during the execution of this new process improvement.

1. Get the key players involved and visible during the execution of the plan.

   Not only should they have participated in the elaboration of the plan, key players should be involved and visible during its execution as well. The reason for this is because these leaders who other people will watch to see whether they believe in what is going on and whether or not they should follow suit. And this is what can make or break the new process improvement.

2. Set up a good mechanism to follow up on the plan execution progress.

   It is key to know how things are progressing, both formally and informally.

3. Celebrate milestones.

   Because everyone is going through this with some kind of apprehension until they clearly see the impact on their life at work, never forget to celebrate whenever a milestone is reached.

   For example, organize regular meetings for the entire organization to attend and hear about some intermediate successes at some key milestones, rather than waiting until the end of the project to make only one announcement at that time.

4. Communicate continuously and clearly (to point out the benefits).

5. Fix bottlenecks and problems as quickly as possible.

   The sooner you know about bottlenecks and problems, and the sooner you fix these, the better your chance of success.

6. Resolve political problems (as soon as possible).

   Whether these problems are due to resistance to change or a personality conflict, you should deal with them as soon as possible and before they spoil the good atmosphere.

7. Make everyone feel mobilized and a winner.

   There is nothing more powerful than people's motivation and the feeling of being a winner. So, pay attention to this and remember to make sure that people feel mobilized and like winners in this new environment.

   For example, mention people's names in a public presentation while enthusiastically praising them for their contribution to the team's success.

Summary

This chapter was all about plan execution, how to set up a good structure to follow up on the plan execution, and who has to be part of it. The chapter also introduced the seven characteristics of an effective plan execution.

Chapter 10

Step 6: Inspecting the Implementation's Progress

Why Is Regular Progress Inspection Critical?

Even with the best action plan, if it is not properly executed, it will be only a plan on paper. This is to say that inspection is a very important step in our approach and that it is crucial to know how to keep abreast of the progress of the implementation. It is only under this condition that we can hope for a good result.

Before getting into what is to be reviewed for inspection, one thing worth remembering is that for the inspection to be possible and easy to accomplish, it is important to create a list of good metrics. This will allow us to calculate the difference or deviation from the original goals in order to know what adjustments we should make to put the execution back on track.

What to Inspect

We recommend that you perform an inspection both at the plan (for management) level and at the action item level (for doers) because they complement one another. Without this double level of inspections, we fear that it will be easy to miss details that could provide insight into the true pulse of the execution progress.

In what follows, we will examine what it means to perform an inspection at the plan level and then at the action item level.

At the Overall Plan Level

At this level, you naturally have the plan at the track level (Figure 10.1), which is something the steering committee members may want to look at, given their busy schedule.

While inspecting the execution's progress at the overall plan level, it is appropriate to look into all the risks, whether they were previously identified or just recently popped up, and have them taken care of before the next meeting of the steering committee (Figure 10.2).

You may also want to inspect the budget and its variances (Figure 10.3).

At the Action Item Level

Included in this category is anything from training (Figure 10.4) to project retrospectives.

Next, there are naturally all the retrospectives from all the projects and their iterations, as can be seen in Figures 10.5 and 10.6. Figure 10.5 can be used for all the project retrospectives and Figure 10.6 can be used for the retrospective of the overall plan.

Tracks	Input	In Progress	Done	Comment
1.				
2.				
3.				
4.				
Etc.				

Figure 10.1 Steering committee reporting by track leads.

Risk Identification	Description	Impact	Owner	Mitigation	Status

Figure 10.2   Risk mitigation plan.

	---- Monthly/Quarterly ----			
Capital	Actual	Budgeted	Variance %	Variance
Capital Budget Purchases				
Future Initiatives				
Expenses				
Operations				
Application and Development				
Maintenance				
Grand total				

Figure 10.3   Inspecting the budget variance.

Summary

We explained in this chapter that while the first inspection is important for executive management, the second inspection will be an important complement to the first inspection because it relates to what is going on in the trenches.

Last but not least, this chapter also provided some examples of what should be inspected.

Name:	
Phone number:	
Email:	
Team (QA, TL, CRM, etc.):	
Agile/Kanban training session(s) attended:	
1. What do you find the most interesting from the session(s) you attended? (Agile/Kanban project management, philosophy, twelve practices, Agile/Kanban team structure, etc.?)	
2. What release(s) are you currently working on? If you are not currently working on a release, which special project are you working on? How big is the team?	
3. Beyond your title, what are your current work responsibilities? Please describe in as much detail as you can.	
4. Besides your title, what would you describe your background and skill sets are? (Requirements, GUI design, testing, architecture, project management, etc.)	
5. Would you like to volunteer to be part of the first Agile/Kanban teams to be deployed? What role would you like to play on this new team? (developer, Agile/Kanban project manager, tester, product owner, etc.?)	
6. Do you have any questions related to the initial Agile/Kanban training you just received and the upcoming Agile/Kanban deployment? Please elaborate.	

Figure 10.4   Inspection at the action item level.

7. How long have you been in this current position? What are the pros and cons of your current position? What do you think we could improve or retain from the current practices?	
8. What obstacles do you foresee that could prevent us from successfully deploying Agile/Kanban in our organization?	
9. What recommendations do you think could help us be successful with the upcoming Agile/Kanban deployment to our organization?	

Figure 10.4 (continued)   Inspection at the action item level.

Project	What Went Well	What Did Not Go Well	Lessons Learned	Action Items to Be Implemented
Iteration #1				
Iteration #2				
Iteration #3				
Iteration #4				

Figure 10.5   Project retrospectives.

Project	What Went Well	What Did Not Go Well	Lessons Learned	Action Items to Be Implemented
Project #1				
Project #2				
Project #3				
Project #4				

Figure 10.6   Plan retrospectives.

Chapter 11

Step 7: Adapt the Chosen Action Plan (as Needed)

Almost every company lives in a dynamic environment that requires it to adapt to its surrounding environment, whether it is to survive or to succeed. For this reason, our action plan will also need to be adapted, especially if the organization's goals and/or business environment change.

Different Types of Change

Not every change in the business will require a dramatic change in our action plan. Depending on the nature of the change, the plan may need to be changed, whether at the track level or at the action item level, as seen in Figure 11.1.

Strategic Change

An example of a strategic change is the arrival of a new executive in charge of the business unit with a new business strategy and new goals.

Operational Change

Operational change may include the replacement of someone who has been serving as product owner (PO) on the project with another manager who will become PO instead.

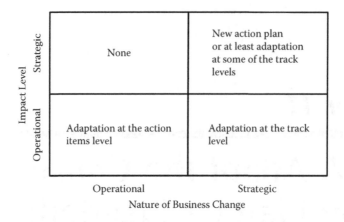

Figure 11.1   Different types of change.

Examples of Adaptations

Strategic Impact

Examples of adaptations of a strategic nature could result in an entire track being dropped. One such example is provided for the current plan as in Figure 11.2 before it is modified to become as in Figure 11.3.

Operational Impact

Examples of adaptations of an operational nature include the following:

> "Client requires that we do not do demo anymore because everything should have been tested and accepted by the users during the cycle."
> "The need is to have more than one PO because no one knows enough of the business to act as the single PO."

From Figures 11.4 and 11.5, we can see that whereas all the tracks are intact, some of their action items have been dropped (as shown in Figure 11.5) to be more in line with the new direction.

Summary

Several examples were provided in this chapter to illustrate the nature of different types of changes to the original action plan.

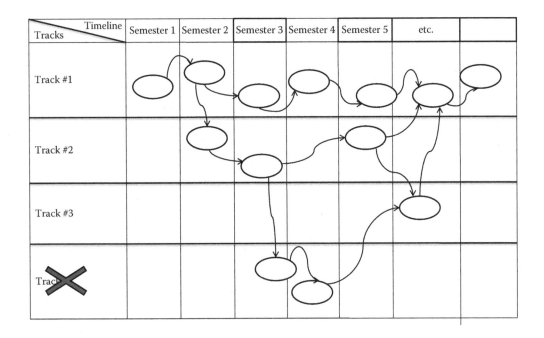

Figure 11.2   Timeline for the action plan—strategic impact.

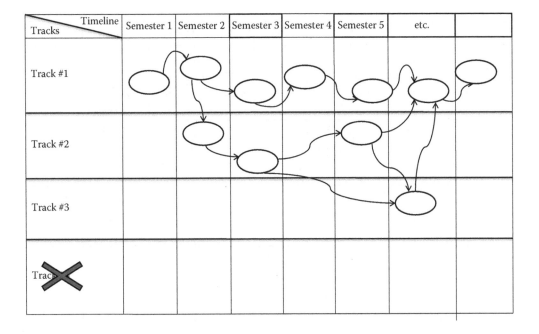

Figure 11.3   Modified timeline for the action plan—strategic impact.

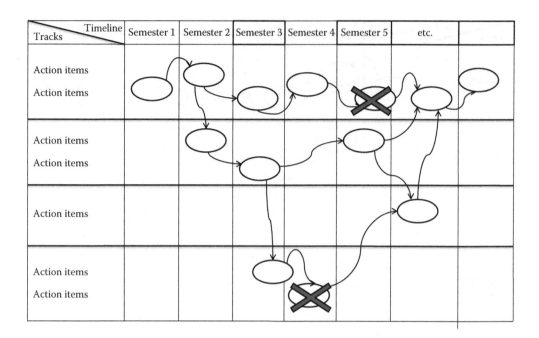

Figure 11.4 The current action plan—operational impact.

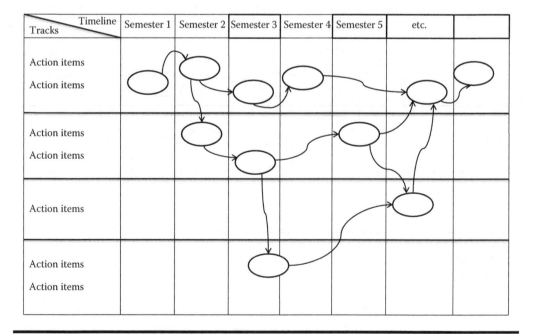

Figure 11.5 The modified action plan—operational impact.

RETROSPECTIVES

Chapter 12

Lessons Learned

Although it may not be possible to make an inventory of all the lessons learned from all the implementations, this chapter lists the main ones that can increase—or decrease—your chance of plan execution success.

1. Not enough focus on change management

   While some people are rightly excited about the new Agile (Scrum) or Kanban (Lean) techniques and practices, one of the most striking mistakes is to forget to include them into a broader perspective of change management—that is, how the change will impact people's careers and work.

2. Not enough (two-way) communication

   Another area where not doing enough can lead to failure is communication—in two directions. Every time something new, whether it is a new process or a new practice, is introduced into an organization, people feel threatened, at least at the beginning. This is why you should solicit feedback from the workers for how they feel and what questions they have about the new process implementation effort.

3. No sense of urgency

   Another obstacle to successful implementation of process improvement is the lack of a sense of urgency. What this means is that people often consider the new process improvement effort as another fad brought in by, and in favor of, management to give management an excuse to justify their pay, to lay off personnel, or both.

   This explains why employees do not normally feel the sense of urgency to do anything quicker, unless top management makes it clear to the workers that this is not just for management's benefit, but for the company's survival or chance of success.

4. No clear and measurable goals

Another impediment to the successful implementation of the new process improvement effort is the lack of clear and measurable goals. This will, in turn, make the teams' work almost impossible to justify because there is no way to show how much progress the teams would have made up to a certain point.

Like quality management guru W. Edwards Deming used to say, what gets measured gets improved. So, unless you take the time and effort to work with top management to identify clearly tangible goals that can be reached through means of hard metrics, you will be in for some big surprises.

5. The hidden powers that be

One of the most memorable failures we had seen is with one of our past clients who had forgotten to identify "the hidden powers that be." Anyone who has been in an organization long enough knows that besides the official chain of command, there is often another unofficial hierarchy, which is also as powerful. So, pay close attention to this and fix this as soon as possible.

6. No infrastructure for continuous integration infrastructure or automated testing

Despite the fact that most people do not consider engineering or technical practices to be part of the most critical aspect of Agile or Kanban, we have not seen any company where Agile and Kanban can be really successful without a good infrastructure for continuous integration and automated testing. This is because regular delivery is what builds trust with the business community; without good continuous integration and automated testing mechanisms in place, it is very difficult to regularly produce quality working code.

7. Get to know middle management and get them on your side

While it is critical to get top management's blessing and support, if you fail to get middle management on your side, you may be in for some surprises. The reason for this is because middle management is where the "rubber meets the road." What this means is that middle management is where all the action takes place, far away from the corporate board room!

CASE STUDIES

Case Study 1: "Customized Agile Combined with Kanban"

ATP Consulting is a software provider for the banking industry, but 80% of its business comes from what it provides to 5% of repeat customers for whom it does most of the enhancement work.

While it has successfully survived some of the world's worst financial crises, ATP's management also know that they need to improve the way their teams build and deliver software. For this reason, they decided to ask for some external consulting to help improve their software operations.

This is why they contacted Enterprise Software Consulting (ESC), a firm specializing in Agile and Lean (Kanban), to guide them in achieving this search for excellence in software delivery.

Having been in the Agile and Lean business for many years, the team from ESC has learned to advise their client's top management to first identify business goals and measurements to drive the new action plan.

Step 1: Identify Business Sponsor and Her or His Needs and Goals

Without exception, this is the first thing the ESC team also asked ATP management to do. Without hesitation, John Silver, ATP's vice president of financial services, told them that he will call a meeting with his senior staff to work on this, and asked if the ESC consulting team had anything they could provide him with prior to this meeting.

The ESC team sent John Silver a short questionnaire and asked him to review and prepare some answers to send back to them prior to his meeting, which they said they would organize with him and his senior staff.

Business Needs and Goals

1. What do you consider to be the five most important items for your business unit?

    Answer: Business growth, revenue generation, customer service, software capability, software cost.

2. What do you consider to be the five most important items for your business unit in working with IT?

    Answer: More frequent software delivery, software meeting expectations, fewer bugs, more intuitive, less expensive.

3. What are your business needs and goals in general?

    Answer:

    Improve development team's throughput by 10% within a 9-month period.

    Increase maintenance team's throughput by 15% by year end.

    Increase team's workload visibility to 100% within a 6-month period.

4. What are the five most important goals for you in dealing with IT, and especially with IT in software development and maintenance?

    Answer: Same as #2.

5. What are IT's greatest weaknesses in supporting your business needs and goals?

    Answer: Long to deliver, not enough features, not always meeting business requirements, high cost.

6. In what areas do you think IT is most effective in helping you achieve your needs and goals?

    Answer: Services and desire to improve.

7. What is the timeline you would like to see for this IT improvement effort?

    Answer: As soon as possible. Otherwise, it will be great if they could align their improvement with our goals.

Figure CS1.1 Answers to the assessment questionnaire.

Figure CS1.1 shows the questionnaire, along with the answers that John Silver sent back to the ESC consulting team. From these answers, they also used the fishbone diagramming technique to break down some of the goals and sub-goals into more detail, as can be seen in Figures CS1.2 and CS1.3.

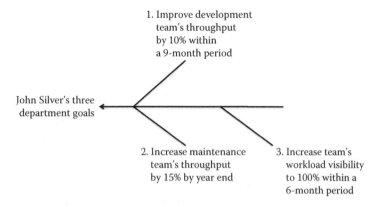

Figure CS1.2   John Silver's three main goals.

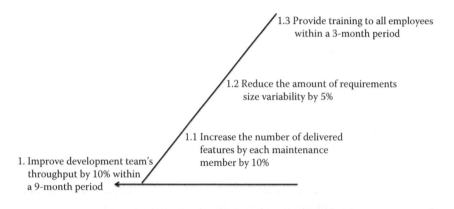

Figure CS1.3   Goal #1 with three sub-goals

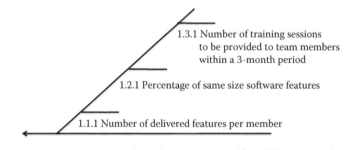

Figure CS1.4   Measurements for the three sub-goals of goal #1.1.

What they were hoping, in doing this, was that they would later on be able to deduct from these the types of action items that should be put in place to remedy the current situation's weaknesses, given the stated goals. In continuing with their diagramming work, they were able next to identify three measurements for the three previous goals, as can be seen in Figure CS1.4.

Goals	Sub-goals	Measures
1. Improve development team's throughput by 10% within a 9-month period	1.1 Increase the number of delivered features by each maintenance member by 10%	1.1.1 Number of delivered features per member
	1.2 Reduce the number of requirements size variability by 5%	1.2.1 Percentage of same size software features
	1.3 Provide training to all of the employees within a 3-month period	1.3.1 Number of training sessions to be provided to team members within a 3-month period
2. Increase maintenance team's throughput by 15% by year end	1. xxxx	1. xxxx
	2. xxxx	2. xxxx
	3. xxxx	3. xxxx
3. Increase team's workload visibility within a 6-month period	1. xxxx	1. xxxx

Figure CS1.5 Goals and sub-goals along with their measurements.

For clarity, they put all the goals and sub-goals, along with their measurements, into the table shown in Figure CS1.5, where we show a portion of their work for illustration purposes only.

Step 2: Perform ATP's Environment Boundary Identification and Assessment

ATP Process Improvement Effort's Boundary

Following the identification of the business problems and the goals that top managers were looking to solve, the next step the team from ATP did with the help from the ESC team was to identify the boundary of this improvement effort.

From what was discussed, it seems like John Silver wanted the effort to be focused on his organization on the U.S. side first (as in Figure CS1.6).

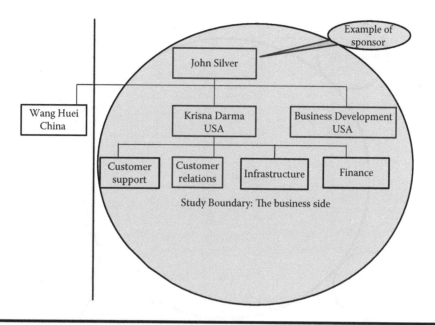

Figure CS1.6 John Silver's organization.

Viewed from another angle, the reporting structure to be assessed would look like the one in Figure CS1.7.

Environment Assessment

Following the identification of the environment to be assessed, question-naires (Figures CS1.8 and CS1.9) were sent to the staff. A sample of the answers that were provided is shown in Figure CS1.9.

Findings Summary

In reviewing the answers to this questionnaire, we can sum up the findings into what follows. As we try to identify scenarios and ultimately the final action plan, we will keep these in mind to serve as the target for our plan.

1. Specialists' culture within ATP
2. Lack of visibility into team's workload
3. A lack of interaction with the business client
4. Some unhappiness about the team's lack of a good estimate
5. Client is somewhat concerned about the number of tickets being taken care of for every release
6. Release dates are often missed
7. A strong architectural background

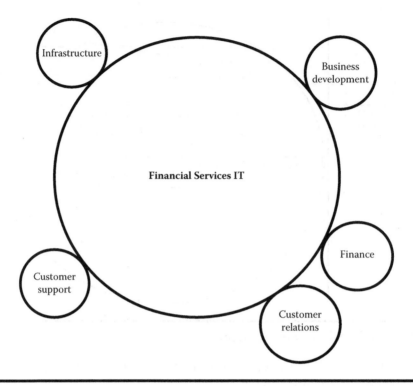

Figure CS1.7 Another view of John Silver's organization to be assessed for this effort.

Organization

1. Describe the business organization under your direction or of which you are a part.
2. How do you interact with IT on a project?
3. Do you have all the resources needed to carry out a project? Please describe.
4. What are the strongest points of your team in your interaction with IT?
5. What are the weakest points of your team in your interaction with IT?
6. Have you ever received any criticism or praise from IT for your team? Please describe.
7. What would you do to improve the collaboration with IT?
8. How would you restructure the organization if you were given the opportunity to do so?

Figure CS1.8 Satisfaction Assessment Questionnaire for the business side.

Team

1. How is the team under your direction organized?
2. How do your team members work together with IT on a project or on a maintenance request?
3. How familiar is your team with Agile concepts?
4. How familiar is your team with Lean concepts?
5. Which people know Agile the best?
6. Which people know Lean concepts the best?
7. Is there anyone you would consider to be a potential problem?
8. How would you restructure the team if you were given the opportunity to do so?

IT Process

1. What do you know about the current IT software process for development?
2. What do you know about the current IT software process for maintenance?
3. Who represents your area in working with IT?
4. What are the strongest points of the IT development process?
5. What are the strongest points of the IT maintenance process?
6. What are the weakest points of the IT development process?
7. What are the weakest points of the IT maintenance process?
8. How would you like to improve the IT development and maintenance processes if you were given the opportunity to do so?

IT Organization

1. How is (are) the IT unit(s) you work with organized?
2. What do they normally need from your team?
3. In what areas have you been the most appreciative of their team? Please describe.
4. In what areas have you been the most negative of their team? Please describe.
5. Whom from the IT unit(s) has your team interacted with the most?
6. How would you qualify that interaction? Negative? Positive?
7. How would you qualify the level of knowledge of the IT unit(s)?
8. What changes would you make to the IT unit(s) to make your working with them even more effective? Please describe.

Figure CS1.8 (continued)   Satisfaction Assessment Questionnaire for the business side.

ATP Enterprise Process Implementation Assessment

Organization

1. Describe the organization under your direction.

   Answer:

   a. Organized along technical specialty with all employees having the same title reporting to a manager over that area, such as business analysis, GUI design and test, etc.

   b. The second line of organization is around client's work

2. How do you interact with the business or IT on a project?

   Answer:

   a. Mainly through the interaction with the business users

   b. Client's product direction is given to us by the project sponsor

   c. Some unhappiness from the client about our technical team estimate (due to lack of good decomposition)

   d. Client is somewhat concerned about the number of tickets being taken care of for every release

   e. Release dates are often missed

3. Do you have all the resources needed to carry out a project? Please describe.

   Answer:

   a. Yes, even though there is sometimes difficulty hiring employees with the right skills

   b. Hiring takes a little bit longer than planned, but we have improved

   c. Lack of visibility into team members' workload

4. What are the strongest points of your team?

   Answer:

   a. A strong architectural documentation and background

   b. Very capable professionals

5. What are the weakest points of your team?

   Answer:

   a. Some unhappiness about the team estimate (due to lack of good decomposition)

   b. Release dates are often missed

Figure CS1.9   Satisfaction Assessment Questionnaire for the IT side.

ATP Enterprise Process Implementation Assessment

Organization (continued)

6. Have you ever received any criticism or praise from the business for your team? Please describe.

   Answer:

   a. Not enough throughput

   b. Don't always meet requirements

7. What would you do to improve the collaboration with IT/business?

   Answer:

   a. More teaming

   b. IT needs to learn more about the business domain

8. How would you restructure the organization if you were given the opportunity to do so?

   Answer:

   a. Hire more specialists

   b. A stronger architectural emphasis

Development Infrastructure

1. Please describe your software development and maintenance infrastructure.

   Answer:

   a. Some traditional .Net development toolset

   b. Some beginning of automated testing tool

2. What are your infrastructure's strongest points?

   Answer:

   a. Some good code review and testing already in place

   b. Some beginning of automated testing tool

3. What are your infrastructure's weakest points?

   Answer:

   a. Not a lot of people know about continuous integration

   b. Not having enough testers

Figure CS1.9 (continued) Satisfaction Assessment Questionnaire for the IT side.

ATP Enterprise Process Implementation Assessment

Development Infrastructure (continued)

4. What is your plan to improve your infrastructure? Please describe.

   Answer:

   a. Purchase of a continuous integration platform

   b. Integration with our bug tracking system

5. What have been the biggest problems with your infrastructure?

   Answer:

   a. Specialists' culture within ATP

   b. Most of the work is done for some very large clients

   c. A lack of interaction with the business client

6. What has been the biggest praise for your infrastructure?

   Answer:

   a. Helpful with user testing

   b. Easy to use

7. What team is responsible for infrastructure and how is it organized?

   Answer:

   a. Helpful with user testing

   b. Easy to use

8. How would you restructure the infrastructure if you were given the opportunity to do so?

   Answer:

   a. Integrated environment from one vendor

Team

1. How is the team under your direction organized?

   Answer:

   a. All of our specialists report to their respective managers

   b. We are still very much a command-and-control shop

   c. Our team has a strong architectural background

Figure CS1.9 (continued)   Satisfaction Assessment Questionnaire for the IT side.

ATP Enterprise Process Implementation Assessment

Team (continued)

2. How do your team members work together on a project or on a maintenance request?

   Answer:

   a. We have a software development life cycle (SDLC) that is rather traditional with all the phases, such as requirements, analysis and design, coding, etc., but our team has started to learn how to deliver incrementally

   b. Normally, the team will work under the leadership of one senior specialist

   c. There is some unhappiness about the team estimate

   d. Client is somewhat concerned about the number of tickets being taken care of for every release

3. How familiar is your team with Agile concepts?

   Answer:

   a. Some high level of understanding but no practice

4. How familiar is your team with Lean concepts?

   Answer:

   a. Some people just took a Kanban class, which they think is very promising for our environment

5. Which people know Agile the best?

   Answer:

   a. Some of our doers plus a few project management professional (PMP) project managers

6. Which people know Lean concepts the best?

   Answer:

   a. Some of our managers but with no practice

7. Is there anyone you would consider to be a potential problem?

   a. While there is some excitement about these new Agile and Kanban ideas, there is obviously some concerns from the workers for their job and/or responsibility

8. How would you restructure the team if you were given the opportunity to do so?

   Answer:

   a. Look to you all for suggestions

Figure CS1.9 (continued) Satisfaction Assessment Questionnaire for the IT side.

ATP Enterprise Process Implementation Assessment

Technology and Application

1. What is your development technology stack? Please describe.

   Answer:

   a. Microsoft.net

   b. MVC architecture, well documented using UML

   c. SQL server

2. Is there any change in plan? Please describe.

   Answer:

   a. Infrastructure modernization money has been requested and approved

3. What has been the weakest point of your technology stack?

   Answer:

   a. Some old tools

4. What has been considered the strongest point of your technology stack?

   Answer:

   a. Tool integration

5. What does your team know the most about this technology stack?

   Answer:

   a. All of the tools that are part of the development suite

6. What does your team know the least about this technology stack?

   Answer:

   a. The continuous integration suite and collaboration

7. Is your application architecture visible and/or fully documented?

   Answer:

   a. Yes!

8. What would you do to improve this technology stack if you were given the opportunity to do so?

   Answer:

   a. Tools integration between Agile and development side

Figure CS1.9 (continued)   Satisfaction Assessment Questionnaire for the IT side.

ATP Enterprise Process Implementation Assessment

IT Process

1. What is your current IT software process for development?

   Answer:

   a. Some different versions of SDLC, which hurts the team cross-pollination and resource allocation

   b. Incremental but neither Agile nor Scrum

   c. Lack of tool that would normally allow more visibility into the team's workload

2. What is your current IT software process for maintenance?

   Answer:

   a. Waterfall with specialists

3. Who represents what areas in this process? Please describe.

   Answer:

   a. Requirements, Analysis, Design, Coding, Testing, User Acceptance, etc.

4. What are the strongest points of your development process?

   Answer:

   a. Somewhat incremental—with specializations

   b. Architecture-driven

5. What are the strongest points of your maintenance process?

   Answer:

   a. Waterfall with specialized professionals

6. What are the weakest points of your development process?

   Answer:

   a. Not enough Agile by nature

7. What are the weakest points of your maintenance process?

   Answer:

   a. The result is a somewhat low level of throughput

8. How would you improve the development and maintenance processes if you were given the opportunity to do so?

   Answer:

   a. Unify our processes into one that draws strength from both Lean-Kanban and Agile for the best performance

Figure CS1.9 (continued)   Satisfaction Assessment Questionnaire for the IT side.

ATP Enterprise Process Implementation Assessment

The Business (External Client) N/A

1. How is (are) the business unit(s) you work with organized?

   Answer:

   a. External clients with sponsor and representatives

2. What do they normally need from your team?

   Answer:

   a. Sometimes new developments, but very often continuous enhancement of the current software releases

3. In what areas have they been the most appreciative of your team? Please describe.

   Answer:

   a. From their feedback, our team's gradual improvements (even if we would like it to be much faster and more than it currently is)

   b. The business also likes our application architecture

4. In what areas have they been the most negative of your team? Please describe.

   Answer:

   a. Not enough throughput and long releases

5. Whom from the business unit(s) has your team interacted with the most?

   Answer:

   a. Business reps of the domains

6. How would you qualify that interaction? Negative? Positive?

   Answer:

   a. Average; can be improved much more

7. How would you qualify the level of knowledge of the business unit(s)?

   Answer:

   a. Good, but can be improved much more

8. What changes would you make to the business unit(s) to make your working with them even more effective? Please describe.

   Answer:

   a. Having their members embedded into our project teams

Figure CS1.9 (continued) Satisfaction Assessment Questionnaire for the IT side.

Step 3: Envision ATP Scenarios

Continuing from the previous goal decomposition for ATP, it was now time for the team to move from the goals to the action items in support of those goals, and together, they came up with Figures CS1.10, CS1.11, and CS1.12.

The next step required the most creativity of all by having the team use the type of list of action items (such as the list in Figure CS1.13) to look at different ways to create cohesive scenarios that would hit most, if not all, of the goals.

Figure CS1.14 shows three scenarios the ESC team generated for ATP management to review, given the department's goals and the result of the assessment.

As originally conceived, the soccer process framework is a process flow that will work for larger teams of approximately eleven people. Without

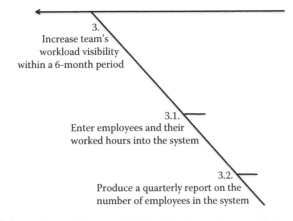

Figure CS1.10   Another example of goal decomposition (goal #3).

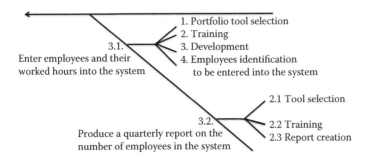

Figure CS1.11   From goals to action items.

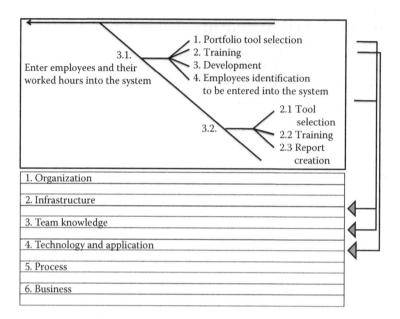

Figure CS1.12   From all (sub-)goals to all action items.

getting into all the details of this new process framework, let's say that it is a process framework that integrates both Agile and Lean techniques and that is intended for both development and maintenance work, as can be seen from Figures CS1.15, CS1.16, and CS1.17.

Lastly, since this is a framework, you will be able to adapt it to your environment to get it to work for you (which will be detailed in another book to come).

Step 4: Develop the Detailed Action Plan for ATP

From the results of the assessment and discussion about the three scenarios, action items were devised by the consulting team and ATP top management and key players, as shown in Figure CS1.18.

As recommended in Chapter 8 of this book, the consulting team and the ATP team worked together to divide the action items around a few tracks (as in Figure CS1.19) in order to achieve a maximum of mobilization of the troops, both for their contribution and buy-in into the plan.

Next, in order to better visualize the action items' dependencies over the time horizon, the consulting and ATP team decided to put the action plan into a timeline, as in Figure CS1.20, and followed the budget, as in Figure CS1.21.

Organization

1. Keep the specialists' culture.
2. Reorganize the team by product line architecture.
3. Keep team size at around twelve people.
4. Hire more QA personnel specialized in automated testing.

Development Infrastructure

1. Set up a new development and support infrastructure, at least in terms of continuous integration, automated testing.
2. Reinforce development server clusters.
3. Build automated test cases.

Team Knowledge

1. There seems to be a gap in knowledge between the development and maintenance team.
2. There is good team knowledge about the architecture.

Technology and Application

1. Make the architecture more visible by documenting it.
2. Keep the current technology.

Process (as can be seen in Figure CS1.17)

1. Combine Agile and Kanban into an unified process with a team size of around eleven or twelve people (like in a soccer team or in the Navy Seals team), which is somewhat larger than the traditional Agile or Scrum team.
2. Combine the first two phases into one (Requirements/Analysis Design and Coding).
3. Incorporate user acceptance testing into the process.
4. No demo will be needed if we incorporate ATTD into the process.
5. The product owner will not be part of the team, but will represent the client outside of the team.
6. The development will have actual business users embedded into their teams.

Business

1. Train the clients' business users to the process.
2. Require that they be available throughout the project life cycle.
3. Reorganize the different releases around architectural platforms.
4. Only produce features that are truly needed by the business ("pull system").
5. Express concern over the lack of knowledge of the new release of the maintenance team.

Figure CS1.13   Action items derived from the goals.

Scenarios	High-Level Description	Action Items	Risks
Scenario #1	Scrum		1. Possible rejection due to the culture of specialists 2. Possible rejection due to new roles that may make people feel threatened 3. Majority of this company's work is maintenance rather than new development 4. The client requires that architecture be visible and get approved by them first due to the presence of their Enterprise Architecture (EA) team
Scenario #2	Kanban		1. Not enough interaction with the business users throughout the life cycle 2. Estimate is required by client, but not recommended by Kanban 3. Iteration is still required by the clients in most of the cases 4. Architecture is required to be visible quickly due to the client's EA

Figure CS1.14   Scenarios.

Scenarios	High-Level Description	Action Items	Risks
Scenario #3	Combination of Agile and Kanban (Lean) + architecture vision (called the soccer process framework, as summarized from Figure CS1.15 to Figure CS1.17.)	1. Kick-off 2. Customer presentation 3. Revise the way we have been doing release planning 4. New way of writing user requirements 5. Evaluate infra-structure tools 6. Etc.	1. Need very good training and well-documented process 2. Need coaching before teams can fly on their own 3. Need some more future reference

Figure CS1.14 (continued)   Scenarios.

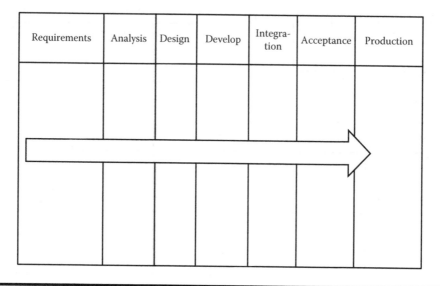

Figure CS1.15   Maintenance process flow.

Requirements	Analysis Design	Review	Development	Acceptance	Deployment

Figure CS1.16   Development process flow.

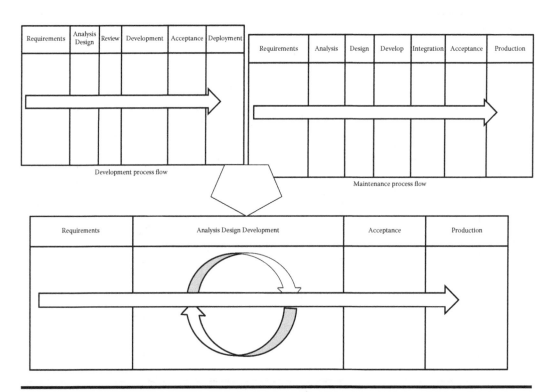

Figure CS1.17   A unified software delivery process flow.

Organization

1. Keep the by-product line architecture.

2. Team size at around twelve people.

Infrastructure

1. Set up a new development and support infrastructure, at least in terms of continuous integration, automated testing.

2. Build automated test cases.

Team Knowledge

1. Spread team knowledge about architecture.

2. Cross-train.

Technology and Application

1. Keep the current technology.

Process

1. Combination of Agile and Kanban.

2. Combine the first three phases into one (Requirements/Analysis Design and Coding).

3. No demo.

4. The development will have actual business users embedded into their teams.

Business

1. Require that they be available throughout the project life cycle.

Figure CS1.18   Derive the action items.

Being careful, the team also ensured that the plan had all seven qualities of a good action plan as discussed in Chapter 8.

1. Have clear business goals (which the plan is intended to support)
   Yes.

2. Logical and easy to understand
   Yes.

3. Organized around small chunks of achievable results
   Yes.

Detailed Action Plan

Action Items	Management Track (#1)	Release Planning Track (#2)	Infrastructure Track (#3)	Organization Track (#4)	Wastes and Bottlenecks Track (#5)	Production Support Track (#6)	Customer Track (#7)
			Internal Track				
1. Kick-off	x						
2. Customer presentation	x						x
3. Revise the current way of doing release planning		x					
4. New way of writing user requirements		x					
5. Evaluate continuous integration (CI) tools			x				
6. Etc.					x		

Figure CS1.19 Detailed action items.

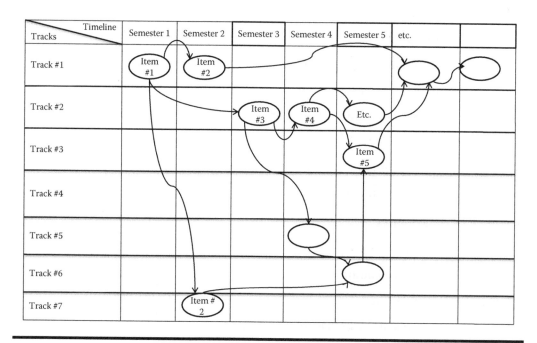

Figure CS1.20   Timeline for the detailed action plan.

4. Clearly identify roles and responsibilities (especially for key people)
   Somewhat.

5. Short and clear milestones
   Yes.

6. A good motivator
   Need to improve.

7. A winning plan
   Despite their careful planning, as it turned out, not everything was going to be perfect during execution of this plan, as seen in the next section.

Step 5: Execute the ATP Action Plan

To execute the plan, the ATP management team decided that they would set up a steering committee composed of John Silver and two of his vice presidents, Jerry Tam and Andrew Burrows, who were in charge of software development and software support/maintenance, respectively.

To ensure a large representation, Jerry Wong, the director in charge of the project management office (PMO), was also invited to sit on the steering

Capital	
Capital budget purchases	
• Automated testing tool	$523,000
• Continuous integration	$124,400
Future Initiatives	
• Action item #1	
• Action item #2	
Expenses	
Operations	
• Consulting	$242,000
• Hiring	$1,000,203
Application and Development	
• Action item #1	
• Action item #2	
Maintenance	
• Version control upgrade	$56,604
Grand total	$1,945,807

Figure CS1.21   Budget for ATP action plan.

committee, in charge of coordinating between the action plan doers and the steering committee for everything that relates to the plan's progress (as in Figure CS1.22).

Last but not least, the Agile and Kanban (Lean) coach, Andrew Locker, was also asked to be part of the steering committee.

As things progressed, the steering committee realized that the previous structure did not provide direct contact between the "doers" and the steering committee; thus it was decided that the PMO would no longer serve as an intermediary between the steering committee and the doers in the new structure (as in Figure CS1.23).

At the same time, it was also decided that track leaders would report their track progress to the steering committee using the format shown in Figure CS1.24.

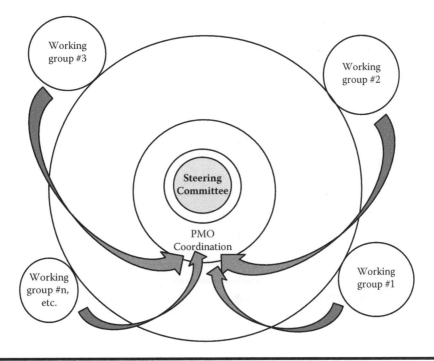

Figure CS1.22   Original organization for the follow-up.

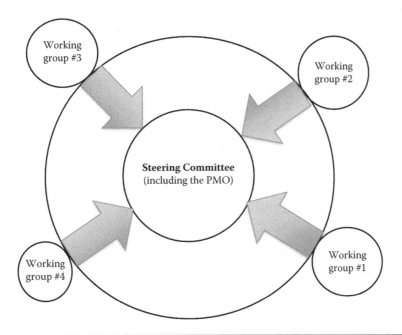

Figure CS1.23   Modified organization for the follow-up.

	Action Items	In Progress	Done	Comment
Tracks				
A. Management track				
B. Release Planning track				
C. Infrastructure track				
D. Organizational track				
E. Etc.				

Figure CS1.24   Track progress reporting.

Step 6: Inspect ATP Execution's Progress

Despite all the care ATP took to get organized for the action plan execution, they realized that nothing could replace the regular inspection of the actual progress of the implementation itself.

For ATP, the following are the items they focused on to keep track of the pulse of the implementation:

1. Identify and mitigate risks.
2. Organize effective retrospectives and learn from their lessons.
3. Inspect the actual budget to watch out for variance.
4. Watch out for positive—and less than positive—changes regarding the different dimensions (of the assessment).

Identify and Mitigate Risks

Like any experienced business team, the management team from ATP knew that with every action item there was also a risk of non-realization. This is why they attached a lot of effort to identifying all the risks of non-realization, as can be seen in Figure CS1.25. In doing this, they also wanted to identify all the potential problems that may happen to ensure that they will never materialize.

Action Items	Risk ID	Risks Description	Impact	Mitigation Plan	Owner
1. Kick-off	Mag01	The kick-off does not go as expected— communication not well received or understood	Extremely high if not properly executed	Test drive with the key actors two days before the actual meeting	Steering committee
2. Customer presentation	Cust01	Inability to increase client's trust in our future ability to deliver	Extremely high— loss of business	Early contact and all participants scheduled to be cleared one week ahead of schedule + rehearsal	Customer relation manager
3. Revise the current way of doing release planning	Rel01	Inability to convince the client's release team that we will need to change the way we have been doing release planning	Extremely high impact—loss of business	Contact to be made quickly with the client's release team and have the coach walk them through our new process To get their reaction and contribution	PMO director

Figure CS1.25   Track progress reporting.

Action Items	Risk ID	Risks Description	Impact	Mitigation Plan	Owner
4. New way of writing user requirements	Req01	Inability to improve the way the business has been writing requirements, which contain a lot of ambiguity	Very high—software not meeting requirements and needs to be reworked	Have the coach to provide early training and practical examples from our own situation to the business	Vice president of development
5. Evaluate CI tools	Infra01	Impossibility to effectively roll out Agile and/or Lean	High—The roll-out may need to be deferred	Avoid lengthy evaluation—just ask for two or three names and pick one of them after some quick meeting with the leads	PMO manager
6. Etc.		Etc.	Etc.		

Figure CS1.25 (continued)   Track progress reporting.

Retrospectives Iteration # xxx				
What Went Wrong	*Action Items*	*Owners*	*Status*	*Comment*
1. The users did not spend enough to test	1.1 Explain the problems that come with this to the business with regard to software quality 1.2 Take action with management to ask for their support to have users dedicate more time to do testing	Lead business analyst (BA)	In progress	Positive meeting with the users
Etc.				

Figure CS1.26 Track progress reporting—retrospective.

Organize Effective Retrospectives and Learn from Their Lessons

Aside from the action items outside of all the projects, it is well known that for all the projects, knowing how to organize their retrospectives and learn from their lessons is very important.

Rather than letting people say something vague like "Yes, everything went well," the ATP management team wanted to make sure that everyone would be specific as to what worked well and what did not.

By the end of the meeting, for every item that did not go well, a correction action would be assigned to an owner, who will work on proposing a solution for the next iteration of the project or for the next project that would work better for the team, as can be seen in Figure CS1.26.

Inspect the Actual Budget to Watch Out for Variance

Like any business-driven company, the ATP management team was also sensitive to how much money they were spending on the plan execution. This is why they also kept an eye on the evolution of the budget, which, from what we can see in Figure CS1.27, shows that ATP ended up spending less than what they thought they would.

Capital	Budgeted	Actual
Capital budget purchases		
Automated testing tool	$523,000	$467,500
Continuous integration	$124,400	$123,960
Future initiatives		
Action item #1		
Action item #2		
Expenses		
Operations		
Consulting	$242,000	$230,940
Hiring	$1,000,203	$1,000,258
Application and development		
Action item #1		
Action item #2		
Maintenance		
Version control upgrade	$56,604	$54,493
Grand total	$1,945,807	$1,877,151

Figure CS1.27   Actual budget for the action plan.

Watch Out for Positive (and Less than Positive) Changes Coming from the Different Dimensions

At the same time ATP tried to identify risks, learned from their project retrospectives, and watched the evolution of their budget, they also kept an eye open on the evolution of the different dimensions in order to make all the necessary corrections on time.

Without being exhaustive, Figure CS1.28 gives an idea of how ATP's dimensions evolved over time during the course of this implementation.

Step 7: Adapt the ATP Plan

For ATP, the adaptations are due mainly from (1) the action items and the environment reaction to the action plan in execution, and (2) a big change in business and/or IT strategy with the move to cloud computing, as recently decided by ATP senior management.

Dimensions	Comment
Organization	Some resistance has been observed and reported about certain project managers having difficulty adapting to a servant-leadership model.
	Some observations have been made about the way the PMO used to do estimates that may need to be changed due to the new Agile/Lean process.
	Some question has been raised whether we should create an Agile and Lean center of excellence to help with the transformation.
Infrastructure	
Team	
Technology and Application	
Process	Great feedback about the new combined process (called the soccer process framework) with only a main comment that the client is still concerned that the maintenance team is not knowledgeable enough to take over the application once it has been deployed
Business	Some concern about the maintenance team's knowledge of the business functionality of the application

Figure CS1.28 Dimensions evolution.

Change from the Action Items and the Environment Reaction to the Action Plan

Due to most of the PM's resistance, it was decided by the steering committee to create an Agile/Lean Center of Excellence outside of the PMO to be responsible for spreading the new culture throughout the company. Also, this Agile/Lean Center of Excellence reported to the VP of IT. As to the PMO, its title was changed from PMO to PDO (Project Delivery Office) and it reported to the vice president in charge of software development.

Given the concern as reported by the customers to the ATP management team, the steering committee also decided to embed one member of the maintenance team into any new development project team to help ensure a

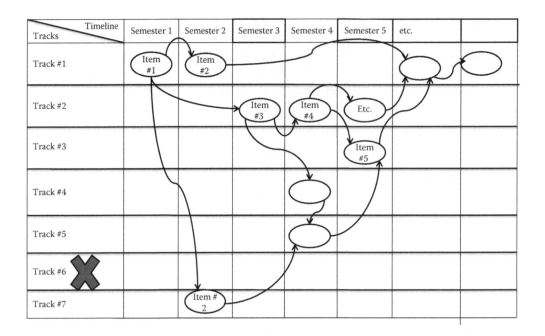

Figure CS1.29 Modified timeline for the detailed action plan.

good transfer of knowledge and a good continuity in terms of maintenance work after the software was released into production.

Change Due to Change in Business and/or IT Strategy

As a consequence of this change, practically the whole track #6 went away (see the infrastructure track in Figure CS1.29).

Lessons Learned

With this case study, one of the biggest lessons learned is that we should never make the assumption that Agile (or Scrum for that matter) is the solution to every single software process problem found in every single company.

Among the first things to do is perform an assessment of the environment and get to know the goals that business and/or IT leaders have for the organization under study in order to have a better understanding as to what is the best action plan for that organization. Even then, expect the action plan to be impacted by any change, whether due to changes in business direction or because of the environmental reactions from the organization to the action items of the plan during its execution.

As you will see, as in this case, sometimes the solution to a software organization is not Agile or Scrum alone, or even Kanban or Lean, but a combination of both, and this in conjunction with some other engineering or architectural practice or knowledge we all have accumulated after many years of experience.

All in all, to be successful in the trenches, we have learned that it is critical to do the following:

1. Get to know the environment and management goals.
2. Listen to feedback from the troops.
3. Always stay open to new ideas.
4. Use proven practices, but always look for creative solutions.
5. Get buy-in from people who are going to use your recommendations or solutions.

Case Study 2: "(Customized) Agile and Kanban Coexistence"

Tax and Financial Services (TFS) just bought Asia Financial Services (AFS), and as part of due diligence they identified that AFS's software organization would need to be combined with TFS's IT under the new name of World Tax Reporting (WTR) under Mary Beckers. This was to equip the newly merged organization with a better IT organization for more effective software delivery and quality of service. They contacted some Agile and Kanban service providers to help them with their endeavor.

One of these firms was Lean and Agile Partners (LAP), very well known for their expertise in Agile and Lean. Unlike many other Lean (Kanban) and Agile service providers, LAP comprised, among its consultants, some of the best professionals in the industry with backgrounds not just in Agile and Kanban, but also in architecture, infrastructure, and software engineering.

Upon landing, the LAP senior consultants were greeted by Jerry Hong, TFS general manager. Hong, known as a man of action, went straight to the main topic of the meeting, which was to increase revenue and cut costs with some result by the end of the first year.

Not losing any more time, he told the consulting team that it would be urgent for them to come up with a plan for Mary Beckers, one of his most important direct reports, who unfortunately had to be out of the office that day due to a family emergency. But, he said, she would be meeting with them the following afternoon. Hong said that Beckers would let them know what her specific goals were, and with his commitment, they would have both his and her backing and funding to make it happen for her growing division, which consisted of approximately 320 professionals.

Step 1: Identify WTR's Business Sponsor and Her Needs and Goals

Mary Beckers's Organization

Figures CS2.1 and CS2.2 provide insight into the WTR organization under Mary Beckers's responsibility.

Figure CS2.3 is another view into Mary Beckers's organization for a phased deployment, which, according to her, should begin with Worldwide Corporate Laws, Sales, and Internal Finance first, before they helped spread the good word to Tax Regulations and Financial Regulations.

In addition, Mary also mentioned that there were two very important projects that she called "pilot projects," which she said she would like to see serve as the sounding board, if successfully executed, for the rest of her organization to learn from.

First Preliminary Training

By experience, the LAP consultants let Mary Beckers know during their meeting the next day that they would like to organize a two-hour online

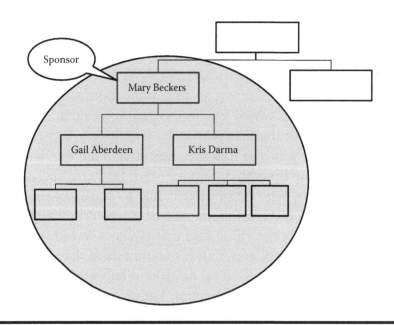

Figure CS2.1   Mary Beckers's organization.

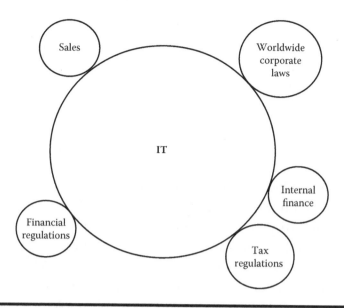

Figure CS2.2   Mary Beckers's organization.

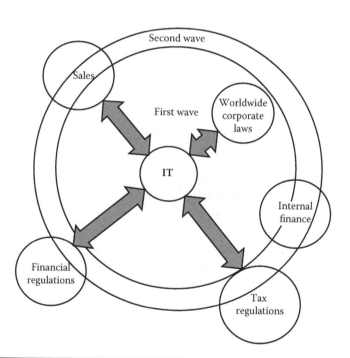

Figure CS2.3   The implementation's boundary and its rolling wave.

introductory presentation to Agile and Kanban to get everyone on board. Right after this, they said they would proceed with an assessment of the organization under her, to begin with the first group of teams that would be impacted by the implementation.

Without hesitation, Mary said that that would not be a problem but, being curious, she asked the consultants to help her understand the goal of such an assessment.

At that time, one of the consultants jumped in to explain that by providing some preliminary understanding and knowledge of Agile and Kanban (Lean), everyone would be on the same page. In other words, he said that the training would provide everyone with a good background to better understand the questionnaire and to make more focused suggestions for the improvement as part of the action plan they were trying to build. This way, the consultant continued, the teams would be more likely to buy into the plan, one of the top conditions for successful acceptance and implementation.

The following is the outline of the presentation the LAP consultants discussed with Mary Beckers.

1. Introduction
    1.2 What Do We Mean by Agile?
        1.2.1 The Agile Manifesto
        1.2.2 Agile Principles and Practices
        1.2.3 Agile Team in Action
            1.2.3.1 Facilitating Factors
            1.2.3.2 Inhibiting Factors
    1.3 What Do We Mean by Kanban and Lean?
        1.3.1 Where Do They Come From?
        1.3.2 More Details on Kanban
            1.3.2.1 Kanban Applied to Software Maintenance
            1.3.2.2 An Example
    1.4 Agile versus Kanban
        1.4.1 Similarities
        1.4.2 Differences
    1.5 The Assessment
        1.5.1 What Is It For?
        1.5.2 The Process and Results
    1.6 Q/A

Goals	Sub-goals
1. Increase software revenue by 5% within one year	1.1 Increase team's throughput by 5% within a year
	1.2 Reduce ideal time by 5% within the first six months
	1.3 Enhance team's estimate capability (due to customers' request) to get to a +/–10 margin
2. Cut software cost by 5% within one year	1.1 Reduce team cost by 5% within a six-month period
	1.2 Increase architecturally reusable assets by 10% before the end of the quarter
	1.3 Reduce rework cost by 10% in six months
	1.4 Enhance team's ability to identify same level of fine grain requirements within the first three months

Figure CS2.4   Goals and sub-goals.

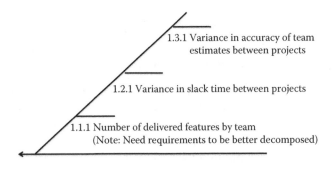

Figure CS2.5   Measurements for the three sub-goals of goal #1.1.

In parallel, some meetings were held to help Mary Beckers and her senior staff start dividing her goal of an increase in revenue and profit margin into more detailed sub-goals (Figure CS2.4).

Figure CS2.5 shows the measurements they came up with for the first three sub-goals for Mary's teams.

For more visibility, the consultant team also put all the goals for the first teams under Mary along with their measurements into a figure that looks like Figure CS2.6.

Goals	Sub-goals	Measures
1. Increase software revenue by 5% within one year	1.1 Increase team's throughput by 5% within a year	1.1.1 Number of delivered features by team (Note: Need requirements to be better decomposed)
	1.2 Reduce slack time by 5% within the first six months	1.2.1 Variance in slack time between projects
	1.3 Enhance team's estimate capability to get to a +/–10 margin (Note: This is a customer's request)	1.3.1 Variance in accuracy of teams' estimate between projects
2. Cut software cost by 5% within one year	1.1 Reduce team cost by 5% within a six-month period	2.1.1 Variance in team cost between projects
	1.2 Increase architecturally reusable assets by 10% before the end of the quarter	2.2.1 Number of reusable assets
	1.3 Reduce rework cost by 10% in six months	2.3.1 Variance in rework cost
	1.4 Enhance team's ability to identify same level of fine grain requirements within the first three months	2.4.1 Variance in actual delivery time for each new requirement

Figure CS2.6   Goals, sub-goals, and measurements.

Step 2: Perform WTR Environment Boundary Identification and Assessment

Given that Mary Beckers had first wanted to focus on World Corporate Laws, Sales, and Internal Finance, all of the World Corporate Laws, Sales, and Internal Finance employees would be part of the first assessment, while people from the Tax Regulations and Financial Regulations areas would be surveyed later.

A summary of answers from the surveyed employees is shown in Figure CS2.7.

Organization

1. Unhealthy relationship between members of several teams

2. There seems to be two separate team organization cultures, one in the software development area where developers seem to enjoy doing everything from gathering requirements to designing to coding, whereas in the maintenance area there seems to be a separation of work along the specialty line (analysts, coders, QA, DBA, etc.)

3. There seems to be a gap of knowledge between development and support as witnessed by the fact that there is no one from the support team who is involved in the development work

4. It has been observed that the business users on development projects are not the same as the users on the maintenance side

5. Most of team members are local to one another (same office)

Infrastructure

1. Good infrastructure with automated testing

2. A good version control system is in place

Team Knowledge

1. Lack of senior level professionals at the expert level

2. Some good level of architecture knowledge but only limited to a few members

Technology and Application

1. The technology stack just got upgraded

2. Application is plenty and fully available via the Intranet

Process

1. Incremental with the UP (Unified Process) in new development but Waterfall in the maintenance area

2. Some heavy documentation

Business

1. Demand for improvement in team estimates

2. Request for improvement in term of requirements gathering for enhancement with the current software release, due mainly to some variations as observed with previous releases

3. Potential acquisition (in negotiation) of another tax software provider in Asia

Figure CS2.7 Answers to the assessment questionnaire.

Step 3: WTR Scenarios Envisioning

Continuing from the previous goal decomposition, it was time for the consultant team and WTR to move from the goals to the search for action items in support of those goals (Figures CS2.8 and CS2.9).

To continue with our illustration, we highlight the three scenarios that WTR management was given to review and vet before they had to decide which scenario, or combination thereof, to choose for their IT-wide process improvement.

From the answers and findings, a summary (Figure CS2.10) was created, which contained all the action items that were being devised to address all the goals previously identified.

Scenarios Risk Analysis

Given management's goals and the results of the assessment, the consulting team, with the help of some leaders, came up with two scenarios for management to review (Figure CS2.11).

Given WTR's specific environment and goals, Mary Beckers and her senior management staff considered scenario #1 as the most likely to meet their needs. This is how they decided to adopt it. Next, to facilitate buy-in from the troops, they also decided that all the action items would be allocated around a few tracks (as in Figure CS2.12), with each one led by a

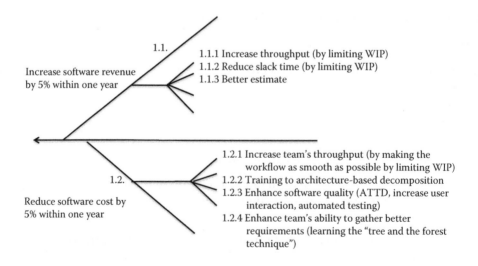

Figure CS2.8   From goals to action items.

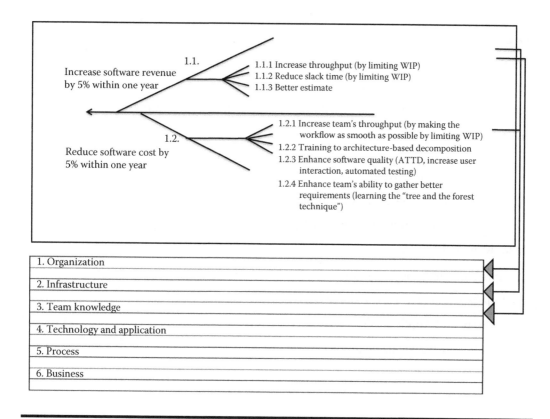

Figure CS2.9   From all (sub-)goals to all action items.

respected leader within her organization, hoping that that would excite and mobilize the teams more easily.

Step 4: Developing the Detailed Action Plan for WTR

Given her strategy, Figure CS2.13 reflects the main lines of Mary Beckers's chosen timeline for WTR action plan.

Figure CS2.14 is the estimated budget the consultants and her management team came up with for Mary Beckers.

Step 5: Execute the WTR Action Plan

Given their specific environment and organizational structure, Mary Beckers asked her project management office (PMO) to take charge of the coordination of the progress of the execution and report everything back to an oversight committee she presided over (as in Figure CS2.15).

Organization

1. Open to Agile structure in new development and Kanban in maintenance.
2. Reorganize the team by product line architecture.
3. Team size can be up to twelve people more or less as they already are.

Infrastructure

1. Improve the current support infrastructure by adding a new continuous integration component.
2. Come up with a better branching strategy.
3. Create a comprehensive regression test suite.

Team Knowledge

1. Spread team knowledge about architecture by cross-training.
2. Improve team's software architecture.

Technology and Application

1. Divide team work along architectural lines.
2. Move into SOA.

Process

1. Agile will be used for new software project while Kanban will be used for maintenance.
2. All requirements will be decomposed to the same level (unlike in traditional Kanban).
3. The product owner will not be part of the team per se but represent the client outside of the team.
4. The development will have actual business users embedded into their teams but not the maintenance teams.
5. Local deployment without any Agile or Kanban automated tool (unless the acquisition is finalized).

Business

1. Train all of the client's business users with the intent to embed some of them into the new process for both new development and maintenance.
2. Require that they be available throughout the project life cycle at least during new development and during the first few phases (requirements, analysis, design, and coding) in maintenance.

Figure CS2.10   From goals to action items.

	High-Level Description	Action Items	Risks
Scenario #1	Enhanced Agile for new development and enhanced Kanban for maintenance	1. Kick-off 2. Modify Agile to include some high-level architecture vision into the Agile process (see Chapters 6 and 7 in Andrew and Phuong-Van Pham's first Agile book, *Scrum in Action*) and modify Kanban to introduce a new technique to gather same level of requirements 3. Train development organization to the new modified Agile process 4. Start pilot project 5. Train Kanban teams to requirements gathering using the "tree and forest" technique 6. Etc.	1. May be resisted by some Agile purists according to whom there should not be any architecture stuff up front, but this is a constraint required by the customer's architecture group 2. Training material and examples must be available on time for this to be successful 3. May need more time to find coaches 4. Examples would need to be ready for this technique to be clear for the participants 5. Potential rejection by people who have heard of planning poker

Figure CS2.11   Scenarios risk analysis.

To ensure the integrity of their product line from an architecture perspective, the following mechanism (Figure CS2.16) was put in place for WTR worldwide product development.

Step 6: Inspect Progress of the WTR Action Plan

Despite all the care Mary Beckers and her staff took to get organized for the action plan execution, they also realized that nothing can replace the inspection of the actual progress of the implementation itself.

	High-Level Description	Action Items	Risks
Scenario #2	Agile	1. Introduction to Agile 2. Training to Agile 3. xxxxx	1. Agile does not seem to fit into our maintenance environment, especially with all the specialists we have and where there is no user available to work with the team on a regular basis 2. May be rejected due to the fact that the client's team often requires that an architecture, even at high level, be presented up front for them to review and see who it would fit into their enterprise architecture 3. xxxx

Figure CS2.11 (continued)   Scenarios risk analysis.

For WTR, they focused on the following steps to keep track of the pulse of the implementation:

1. Identify and mitigate risks.
2. Lessons from the pilot project's retrospectives.
3. Inspect the actual budget to watch out for variance.
4. Watch out for positive—and less than positive—changes on the different dimensions.

Identify and Mitigate Risks

Like any experienced business team, the management team from WTR also knew that with every action item there was also a risk of non-realization. This is why they attached a lot of effort to identify all the risks associated

Action Items	Management Track (#1)	Process Track (#2)	Internal Track				Customer Track (#7)
			Infrastructure Track (#3)	Organization Track (#4)	Wastes and Bottlenecks Track (#5)	Production Support Track (#6)	
1. Kick-off + introduction to Agile and Kanban	x						x
2. Modify Agile to include some high-level architecture vision into the process and modify Kanban by introducing a new technique to gather same level of requirements		x					
3. Train development team to the new modified Agile process		x					
4. Start development pilot project				x			
5. Train Kanban team to the new requirements gathering technique						x	
6. Etc.					x		

Figure CS2.12 Detailed action plan.

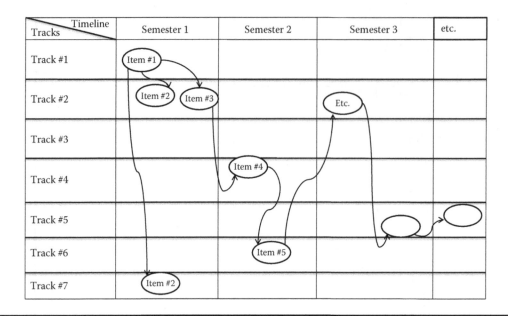

Figure CS2.13   Timeline for the WTR action plan.

Capital	
Capital Budget Purchases	
• Automated testing tool	
• Continuous integration	$224,400
Future Initiatives	
• Action item #1	
• Action item #2	
Expenses	
Operations	
• Consulting	$342,000
• Hiring	
Application and Development	
• Action item #1	
• Action item #2	
Maintenance	
• Version control upgrade	$216,604
Grand total	**$783,004**

Figure CS2.14   Budget for the WTR action plan.

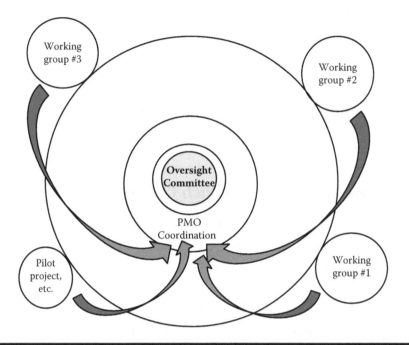

Figure CS2.15   The original organization to follow up on the WTR execution.

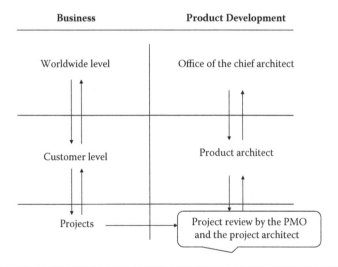

Figure CS2.16   Architecture-based WTR worldwide product development.

with all the action items to ensure that they all were properly executed, and should anything derail them, they would want to identify those potential problems to ensure that they would never happen (Figure CS2.17).

Lessons from the Pilot Project's Retrospectives

Figure CS2.18 shows some lessons drawn from the initial pilot project.

Inspect the Actual Budget to Watch Out for Variance

Like any business-driven leader, Mary Beckers was also sensitive about how much money she would spend on the plan execution for WTR. This is why she also kept an eye on the evolution of the budget, which we can see in Figure CS2.19.

Watch Out for Positive—and Less than Positive— Changes on the Different Dimensions

At the same time that WTR identified risks, learned from their project retrospectives, and watched their budget evolution, they also kept an eye on the evolution of the different dimensions to make all the necessary corrections on time.

Figure CS2.20 gives us an idea of how the WTR's dimensions evolved over time during the course of implementation.

Step 7: Adapt the WTR Action Plan

For WTR, the adaptations are due mainly to (1) the action items and the environment reaction to the action plan in execution, and (2) a big change in business and/or IT strategy with the acquisition of a software company in India.

Changes Coming from the Action Items and the Environment Reaction to the Action Plan

Organizational

Upon suggestions from the local development teams, the worldwide enterprise architecture team agreed to create some local architecture teams to

Action Items	Risk ID	Risks Description	Impact	Mitigation Plan	Owner
1. Kick-off	Mag01	The kick-off does not go as expected—communication not well received or understood	Extremely high if not properly executed	Test drive with the key actors two days before the actual meeting	Oversight committee
2. Modify Agile to include some high-level architecture vision into the process and modify Kanban by introducing a new technique to gather same level of requirements	Arch01	Inability to find enough people with the right expertise	High	Early hiring	Worldwide Product Architecture
3. Train development team to the new modified Agile process	Pro02	Inability to finish the enhancement on time and get people's busy schedules cleared up for attendance	Extremely high impact	Get early management's approval for schedule clearing	PMO
4. Start development pilot project	Pro03	Inability to put a team together on time	High	Get Mary Beckers's approval	PMO
5. Train Kanban team to the new requirements gathering technique	Sup01	Get attendees' schedules cleared up	High—the roll-out may need to be deferred	Early approval from management	PMO
6. Etc.		Etc.	Etc.		

Figure CS2.17   Risk mitigation.

Retrospectives				
Project: xxx Iteration # xxx				
What Went Wrong	*Action Items*	*Owners*	*Status*	*Comment*
1. Some user stories were still too big or too small	1.1 Augment training material with exercises 1.2 Test by the end of the training 1.3 Ask for participants' feedback	Lead Business Analyst (BA)	In progress	Good feedback for the new training
Etc.				

Figure CS2.18   Retrospective.

Capital	Budgeted	Actual

Capital budget purchases
    Automated testing tool
    Continuous integration
	$224,400	$223,960

Future initiatives		
Action item #1 Action item #2		
Expenses		
Operations		
Consulting Hiring`	$342,000	$553,940
Application and development		
Action item #1 Action item #2		
Maintenance		
Version control upgrade	$216,604	$154,493
Grand total	$783,004	$932,393

Figure CS2.19   Budget (negative) variance for the WTR action plan.

Dimensions	Comment
Organization	Some resistance has been observed, but essentially the troops do buy in to the new processes and everything goes well.
Infrastructure	N/A
Team Knowledge	N/A
Technology and Application	Great job by the worldwide architecture team for making it easier on the teams by decentralizing their architectural review.
Process	Great feedback about the new processes.
Business	Quite positive, but with some clear need for us to do a better job at providing a more accurate estimate for their maintenance/enhancement request. This, in turn, will require that we do a better job at decomposing requirements into the same level of details for a better estimate.

Figure CS2.20   Dimension evolution.

facilitate the reviews and working relationships between people in the same time zone and location.

Process

Upon the clients' requests, it was agreed that a more objective estimation technique will be created to help the clients verify our estimates and improve their own budgeting.

The same way it was decided to create a more objective estimation technique, for clients' verification, it was also decided to use a new requirement technique that would allow teams to identify more easily user requirements and dissect them to more or less the same level of detail to enable a better estimate.

To help Kanban team members and managers know how long someone has been working on an item, it was decided that some modifications will be added to the Kanban card to show how long someone has been working on an item, as can be seen in Figure CS2.21.

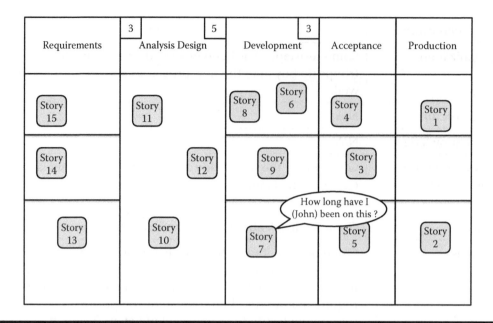

Figure CS2.21   How long have you been in this state?

Change Due to Change in Business and/or IT Strategy

As a consequence of the acquisition of a new software company from India, a new track with its own action items were added to the action plan as in Figure CS2.22.

A new budget was drawn up to take into account the cost of the execution for the new software company (Figure CS2.23).

Lessons Learned

With this case study, the lessons learned are that our process solution may be different depending on whether it is for new software development or maintenance. Agile (Scrum) and Kanban (Lean) do not have to exclude one another but can coexist for the benefit of all, such as what the Wikispeed team did with their remarkable high-speed car prototype.

As always, among the first things we shall do is to perform an assessment of the environment and get to know the goals of business and/or IT leaders, in order to have a better understanding of what would constitute the best action plan for that organization. Even then, expect, once again,

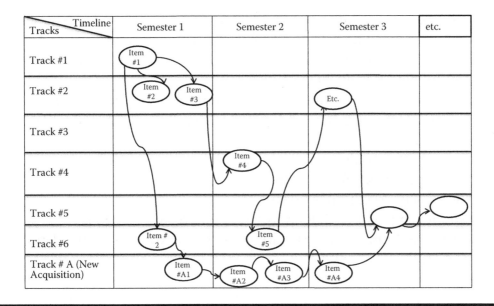

Figure CS2.22   Mary Beckers's timeline for the WTR action plan.

Capital	New Budget		

Capital budget purchases
    Automated testing tool
    Continuous integration
	$524,400		

Future initiatives			
Action item #1 Action item #2			
Expenses			
Operations			
Consulting Hiring	$742,000		

Application and development
    Action item #1
    Action item #2			

Maintenance Version control upgrade	$416,604		
Grand total	$1,683,004		

Figure CS2.23   New budget for the WTR action plan following the acquisition.

the action plan to be impacted by any change, whether due to changes in business direction (like the acquisition of a new company from India) or because of the reactions from the organization's ecosystems to the action items of the plan during its execution.

All in all, it is a good reminder to remember that in order to be successful with process changes in the trenches, we have to learn to do the following:

1. Know the environment and management goals.
2. Listen to feedback from the troops.
3. Always stay open to new ideas.
4. Use proven practices, but always look for creative solutions.
5. Get buy-in from people who are going to use your recommendations or solutions.

APPENDICES

V

APPENDICES

V

Appendix A: From the Project Management Office to the Project Delivery Office

It has become rather fashionable to suggest that the project management office (PMO) should become, with the transition to Agile and to Lean, the portfolio management office. However, there are many types of PMO, with some having a mission that is more or less operational or strategic and some having a more supporting than controlling role (as can be seen in Figure A.1).

So, unless your organization's PMO is in the upper right-hand quadrant of Figure A.1, suggesting that the PMO should become the portfolio management office is a step that many organizations and their PMOs will not be ready to take or should not take.

Instead, what we recommend is that the PMO eventually change its name from PMO to project delivery office (PDO) to acknowledge the fact that it should no longer manage projects, but only help facilitate the delivery of projects by project teams. This should, when there is no change in the PMO's mission, help account for the new nature of Agile (and Lean) project management, with development teams becoming more self-organized and empowered.

Besides the eventual name change, we also think the following two items should change with the new implementation with Kanban (Lean) and Agile (Scrum):

1. The project manager's job description
2. The way the PMO calculates its project estimate

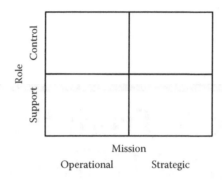

Figure A.1   Different types of PMO

Modify the Traditional Project Manager's Job Description

Project Manager's Traditional Job Description

Provide direct management and leadership to the project team. The project manager has the responsibility to take the necessary action to see that the projects are completed efficiently, on time, and within budget (plus or minus 5%).

Work closely with the assigned project team members to determine their appropriate roles and responsibilities. Review the project financial statements and develop a comprehensive project plan and schedule for the project team.

Once the project's overall scope, cost, and high-level timeline have been determined and approved, develop a detailed project budget, cash flow, and project schedule.

Ensure that the project plan is executed according to the plan's details to meet the business unit's strategic plan.

Close out the project before team members are assigned to a new project.

Agile/Lean Project Manager's New Job Description

Progressive company looking for an Agile/Kanban (Lean) project manager who will accomplish the following:

Help the project team understand the new Agile or Lean (including Kanban) concepts and practices.

Optimize the team's performance and process by helping the team continuously look for opportunities to reduce wastes and bottlenecks.

Work with the business sponsor to help clarify the product direction and prioritize the iteration backlog.

Enable the development team to self-organize and be empowered to make their own decisions with regard to their commitment.

Help optimize the team's process by organizing iteration and project review for teams to inspect what worked and what did not work.

Remove impediments and obstacles to help the team stay focused and on track toward delivery.

Continuously look for opportunities to get the workflow as smoothly as possible to reduce lead time and to increase throughput.

Continuously foster a culture of continuous improvement, creativity, and innovation.

Keep track of the project's progress and report status back to management.

Change the Way the PMO Calculates Its Project Estimate

Normally, the PMO does its project estimate by always padding some contingency buffer to the original estimate, which, in many cases, increases the cost of the project.

Given the fact that there is more frequent interaction with the business (which should help uncover mistakes and errors sooner rather than later), there will be no more need to pad the project's estimate with contingency numbers. The only precaution we suggest is that while doing the team's estimate, the PMO should remember that the ideal work day is not eight hours but rather six hours or so.

Appendix B: Change Management

As seasoned professionals, we are sure that you have read many books that deal with change management, or you may have even dealt successfully with many of these changes during your career. We are not going to repeat what you may have read or already know too well. The only thing we would like to convey here is that, for any change program to be successful, such as the implementation of new processes that we have been talking about in this book, a change program should include the following seven qualities (Figure B.1).

1. Clear business goals
   Without a clear set of business goals, it is easy to lose focus during implementation.
2. Good leadership
   Make sure that people who are respected within the organization are involved and visible in this effort.
3. A winning proposition
   Make sure that the new enterprise effort can make everyone a winner in that everyone's work will be valued and everyone's skills enhanced.
4. Full commitment
   Make sure that the teams see to it that the leadership team is fully committed to seeing this happen—not just in words but in actions.
5. Supported by a plan
   Having a plan is like having a roadmap, which you can adjust but which will provide you with some kind of constant direction as to where you would like to go.

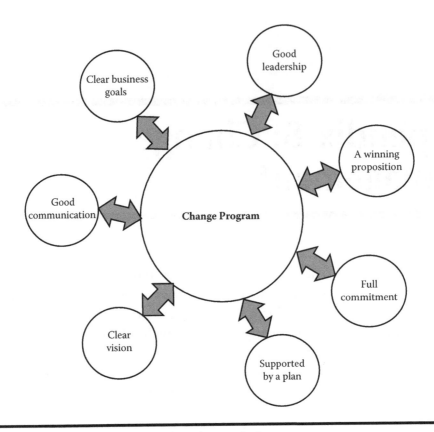

Figure B.1   The seven characteristics of a good change program.

6. Clear vision

Believe it or not, everything has to start with your having a clear vision as to what you would like to accomplish with this process improvement initiative. The clearer your vision is and the better articulated your plan is, the more likely you will succeed in this endeavor.

7. Good communication

We can never emphasize enough that communication is key. So communicate. Communicate to show people what there is for them to work hard on and to contribute to make it happen.

Appendix C: Two Most Important Tools of a Good Software Development Infrastructure

For all the projects we have been on and for all that we have seen, a good software development or maintenance infrastructure can really make a big difference.

Without a good infrastructure in support of Agile (Scrum) and Kanban (Lean), it can be all talk with very little to deliver.

Among all the tools, there are two most important tools we think you must have in place as soon as possible:

1. Continuous integration
2. Automated testing

Continuous Integration

There is no doubt that a regular cadence or delivery will be among the factors that increase customer trust in the team when they transition into Agile (Scrum) and Kanban (Lean). For this reason, the team must have the continuous integration infrastructure in place as soon as possible to allow them to build and deliver on a regular basis.

So, make sure that you include this tool as part of the infrastructure you have set up, preferably even before the organization makes its move into Agile (Scrum) or Kanban (Lean).

Automated Testing

Unless what you build is a small application or very trivial website, it is difficult for teams to develop large-scale software without the help of a good automated testing tool.

Also, given the high number of test cases that have to be run manually every time the team gets ready to deliver a new software release, most teams, if not all, will realize that they need a good tool for automated testing.

So, remember to include this tool in your action plan as something to acquire as soon as possible. You will be glad you did.

Glossary

Adaption: The art of modifying a plan or strategy to make it fit the environment in order to be operational

Agile: A new approach to software development and project management, which recommends that development teams work more regularly with business users during short iterations and that teams should be empowered and self-organized to get their work done

Assessment: The art of identifying an organization's context or environment from different perspectives (dimensions) to have a better grasp of its complexity or situation

Assessment questionnaire: Questionnaire used to perform the organizational assessment

Boundary: The surrounding limits of an organization or of a project

Budget: Financial plan in support of the action plan for process improvement

Business-driven process improvement: Rather than improving software processes for the sake of process improvement, business-driven process improvement is an approach that says that any process improvement can succeed only if it is based on a company's business goals

Business goals: Business objectives to be used as the driving forces for a process improvement effort

Business needs: The needs of a business corporation or unit, which can be translated into a set of business goals

Coordination: The art of integrating different teams' work or teams' tracks into a cohesive action plan for process improvement

Dimensions: Different perspectives of a situation

Envisioning: The art of identifying solutions for an organizational problem that has been identified

Execution: The art of getting things or an action plan to be implemented

Inspection: Action of verification by which action items or activities are verified to see if they have produced the expected results

IT (Information Technology): Name usually used to designate the technology department within a company

Kanban: A new approach to software development using Lean concepts and techniques

Mobilization: The art of motivating people around a common cause

Multi-track plan: Different sub-components of an action plan, the results of which, when put together, will produce the expected results of the overall plan

Objectives (business objectives): Objectives (and goals) to be used to drive an action plan

Planning: The art of conceptualizing a plan

Portfolio matrix: Grid that shows the basket of projects around some chosen criteria

Post-training questionnaire: Questionnaire used to gather feedback from participants in a training class

Program: A set of projects, the result of all of which forms a cohesive one

Project: A human endeavor, the goal of which is to produce a new product or service with a start date and end date

Reporting: Action by which someone is made aware of the progress of an action plan or of a project during regular intervals

Risk mitigation: The art of reducing the impacts of the risk that has been identified

Risks: Elements, either coming from the external environment or from the inside, that could derail an action plan

Roadmap: An action plan that shows the target of what is to be accomplished and what action items should be taken to arrive at the target (expected outcome)

Scenario: A potential solution, or option representing a solution, for an undertaking such as a process improvement effort

Scope: The size or extent of an action plan

Scrum: One of the best-known Agile processes that has proven to be successful where teams of seven to nine people work interactively with business users within short Sprints (iteration) to regularly deliver software increments

SMART goals: Goals that are specific, measurable, achievable, and realistic within a reasonable time frame

Steering committee (governing committee): Group of senior leaders
whose direction and decision are critical to the execution of an
action plan

Working group: Group of people working together on a sub-set of items
as part of a track of a larger action plan

Bibliography

Anderson, David J. *Kanban: Successful Evolutionary Change for Your Technology Business*. Sequim, WA: Blue Hole Press, 2010.

Harvard Business Review on Change. Cambridge, MA: Harvard Business School Press, 1998.

Hibbs, Curt, Steve Jewett, and Mike Sullivan. *The Art of Lean Software Development*. Sebastopol, CA: O'Reilly, 2009.

Japan Management Association, ed. *Kanban Just-in-Time at Toyota*. Translated by David J. Lu. Cambridge, MA: Productivity Press, 1985.

Kendrick, Tom. *Identifying and Managing Project Risk*. New York: Amacom, 2009.

Pham, Andrew, and Phuong-Van Pham. *Scrum in Action: Agile Project Software Management and Development*. Boston: Cengage, 2010.

Poppendieck, Mary, and Tom Poppendieck. *Lean Software Development: An Agile Toolkit*. Boston: Addison-Wesley, 2003.

Sayer, Nathalie J., and Bruce Williams. *Lean for Dummies*. 2nd ed. Hoboken, NJ: John Wiley and Sons, 2011.

Shingo, Shigeo. *A Study of the Toyota Production System from an Industrial Engineering Viewpoint*. Tokyo: Japan Management Association, 1981.

Womack, James, Daniel Jones, and Daniel Roos. *The Machines That Changed the World*. New York: HarperPerennial, 1991.

Index

T - #0663 - 101024 - C0 - 254/178/11 - PB - 9781466557482 - Gloss Lamination